A PLACE CALLED ILDA

A Place Called Ilda

*Race and Resilience at a Northern
Virginia Crossroads*

Tom Shoop

RIVANNA BOOKS
University of Virginia Press
Charlottesville and London

The University of Virginia Press is situated on the traditional lands of the Monacan Nation, and the Commonwealth of Virginia was and is home to many other Indigenous people. We pay our respect to all of them, past and present. We also honor the enslaved African and African American people who built the University of Virginia, and we recognize their descendants. We commit to fostering voices from these communities through our publications and to deepening our collective understanding of their histories and contributions.

RIVANNA BOOKS
An imprint of the University of Virginia Press

Printed in the United States of America on acid-free paper

First published 2024

1 3 5 7 9 8 6 4 2

LIBRARY OF CONGRESS CATALOGING-IN-PUBLICATION DATA

Names: Shoop, Tom, author.
Title: A place called Ilda : race and resilience at a northern Virginia crossroads / Tom Shoop.
Description: Charlottesville : Rivanna Books, University of Virginia Press, 2024. | Includes bibliographical references and index.
Identifiers: LCCN 2023028987 (print) | LCCN 2023028988 (ebook) | ISBN 9780813950860 (paperback ; acid-free paper) | ISBN 9780813950877 (ebook)
Subjects: LCSH: African American cemeteries—Virginia—Ilda—History. | African Americans—Virginia—Ilda—History. | Ilda (Va.)—History. | Ilda (Va.)—Race relations—History.
Classification: LCC F234.I43 S56 2024 (print) | LCC F234.I43 (ebook) | DDC 975.5/291—dc23/eng/20230823
LC record available at https://lccn.loc.gov/2023028987
LC ebook record available at https://lccn.loc.gov/2023028988

Cover art: *Atlas of fifteen miles around Washington, including the county of Montgomery, Maryland.* (Philadelphia: G. M. Hopkins, 1879, © 1878; Library of Congress, Geography and Map Division, D.C., 20540-4650 USA dcu, G1275 .H58 1879)

For Julie

It all fades away but you

CONTENTS

A PLACE CALLED ILDA

Introduction

THE INTERSECTION OF Little River Turnpike and Guinea Road in Annandale, Virginia, twelve miles outside of Washington, D.C., is at first glance—and second and third glances, truth be told—a nondescript slice of suburbia. On one side of the turnpike are neighborhoods made up of groups of ever-larger homes erected in waves of development since the mid-twentieth century. On the other sit a firehouse and a Jewish community center. Down the street are a drugstore, a gas station, and a restaurant.

It would be easy to assume that nothing of particular significance happened here. It would also be wrong.

On the morning of October 4, 1898, Horace Gibson awoke to a familiar, if maddening, scene. Franklin Minor, who lived across the street from the blacksmith shop that Gibson and his friend Moses Parker had built into a successful business, was again causing trouble. This time the issue was property damage caused by Minor's horse.

Gibson and Parker, African American men born into slavery, had developed the community of Ilda from the ground up. They had tangled with Minor, a white lawyer, before. In 1874, Minor was ordered to pay a one-hundred-dollar fine after he was charged with harassing Gibson. Since that time, Minor had developed a habit of threatening his neighbors, both Black and white.

The two were old men now—Gibson, eighty-one, and Minor, seventy-six. But age hadn't cooled Minor's volatile nature or changed Gibson's unwillingness to put up with his dangerous antics. They were inexorably headed toward another confrontation. And the problem may have been compounded by the fact that Minor lived in a house on a piece of property at the corner of Little River Turnpike and Guinea Road that had also been home to a cemetery for enslaved people in the area. That cemetery would survive into the twenty-first century, despite numerous efforts to develop the land on which it sat.

Whether or not the thought that an unstable neighbor occupied hallowed ground factored into Gibson's state of mind that October morning, Minor's could be summed up in one word: violent. Because when the two met, Gibson quickly found himself at the business end of a shotgun.

And just like that, Minor let fly with both barrels. One load of shot tore into Gibson's abdomen, the other into his shoulder.[1] Astonishingly, he would survive. The community he had helped to forge would not.

That didn't bring an end to the controversy at the intersection. On the morning of June 21, 2007, Ray Khattab of Capital Paving, Inc., reported to his job site as usual. Except little was turning out to be usual about the road-widening project at the intersection of Little River Turnpike and Guinea Road.

Already, Khattab had received an anonymous letter attacking the project as encouraging overdevelopment in the area and disturbing a graveyard. Then there was the graffiti on a construction shed warning of the "wrath of God" upon those working on the project.

The intersection of Little River Turnpike and Guinea Road in February 2023. (Photo by the author)

When Khattab arrived, it didn't take long for him to figure out that something else was wrong: Someone had fired a pellet gun at a piece of construction equipment—for the third time. Windshield glass was everywhere, Khattab told a local radio station.

"Someone," he said, "is very upset with the disturbance of that cemetery."[2]

The vandals' effort to stop the construction project failed. More cars than ever—some forty thousand per day—pass through the intersection now, jockeying for position with the fuel trucks heading back and forth from a petroleum storage facility down the road to the west.[3]

What most of the drivers of those vehicles fail to notice is the roadside historical marker that provides a little information about what used to be here: a community that sprang up out of the ruins of the Civil War. Gibson, Parker, and their families succeeded, against all odds, in starting a business that became the focal point of a thriving village. They became significant landowners in the process, and the community grew to have its own church, school, and post office.

Yet it may have disappeared from memory entirely if not for the persistent efforts of two of Gibson's and Parker's descendants more than a century later. They researched and wrote, cajoled government officials, and demanded that what their ancestors built be remembered, respected, and recognized.

The community Gibson and Parker founded was unusual in many ways, not the least of which is that it was racially integrated. That is, until their descendants moved elsewhere. Then the enclave gradually withered away. But traces remained, especially in the small plot of land that contained the cemetery. Its resistance to the development that sprang up around it over the decades was almost supernatural.

Ultimately, when the graveyard succumbed to the unstoppable expansion of suburbia early in the twenty-first century, the resulting controversy served to ensure its name would live on. The lives of the voiceless enslaved people who were forced to work in and around the Little River Turnpike–Guinea Road intersection were made real.

All of this occurred at a time when efforts to preserve African American cemeteries from the onslaught of development—even on a small scale—were rarely successful in Virginia. Not until the second decade of the twenty-first century would that begin to change.

The area in and around the cemetery turns out to have a rich and important story to tell. As Emily Williams writes in *Stories in Stone,* on recovered African American graves in Colonial Williamsburg, "All history is local. It occurs somewhere and is thereby localized. It is as we begin to tie the local stories together that we get regional stories, and as we aggregate those we get national and international narratives."[4]

The intersection of Little River Turnpike and Guinea Road holds keys to understanding the critical factors that shaped the development of the United States: slavery, segregation, religion, transportation, suburban sprawl, war, and peace. It is a place where the American Dream could have and should have become a reality for more than a privileged few.

In this community, a group of people struggled to make a life for themselves with the grand promise of freedom and experienced the harsh reality of its limitations. They lived through seismic shifts that turned their lives upside down, and saw the slow erosion of the illusion of equality. Theirs is a tale that includes horse thievery, attempted murder, savage beatings, hate crimes, hidden human remains—and also involves zoning decisions, real estate covenants, and school board rulings.

It is a story of bondage and liberty, of entrepreneurship and bureaucracy, of optimism and despair, of development and preservation. It is the story of a place called Ilda, and of America.

I

Destruction

A GOOGLE SEARCH FOR "Ilda" yields a lot of interesting information about the International Laser Display Association. But switch to the Maps function and it'll drop a pin at the intersection of Little River Turnpike and Guinea Road. More detailed maps show the Woods of Ilda housing development or the Ilda swimming pool complex.

But nobody ever says they're headed to Ilda to buy some gas, grab some dinner, or get a prescription filled. Because while there's a service station, a sushi spot, and a pharmacy in what was once Ilda, it no longer exists as an actual place. It's a ghost village, living only in memory and a couple of place-names.

But Ilda was once a vibrant community that was literally at the center of life in Fairfax County. Its denizens regularly made both the society and news pages of papers like the *Washington Evening Star,* the *Alexandria Gazette,* the *Fairfax Herald,* and the *Herndon Observer.* And Ilda became a meeting place for citizens to express concerns about everything from road construction to temperance crusades.

Ilda rose from the ashes of Fairfax County after the Civil War. But long before that, it was home to indigenous peoples for thousands of years. "Numerous prehistoric archaeological resources dating to the earliest known human inhabitants of Fairfax County (ca. 9000 B.C.) and later have been identified in . . . this sector and adjacent uplands," Fairfax County researchers concluded in 1991.[1] In the early seventeenth century, the Manahoac tribe populated the area. In an 1870 interview with ethnologist Horatio Hale, a man named Nikhona—also known as Mosquito—said he was the last surviving Manahoac and therefore the rightful owner of Northern Virginia. That's an argument at least as convincing as the English claim of ownership of the land with the establishment of the Virginia Colony in 1607.[2]

After Europeans moved in, the area that eventually would evolve into Ilda became part of Ravensworth, the largest plantation in Fairfax County. Ravensworth would, over time, become a cog in a New World agricultural machine that was heavily dependent on one crop—tobacco—and adhered to one economic principle: manage the labor-intensive cultivation and harvesting process by enslaving people to do the work.

When William Fitzhugh bought the land that became Ravensworth in 1685, it was the largest single land grant in Northern Virginia. Fitzhugh never made his home on the property, instead hiring overseers to live there.

It's difficult to overstate the degree to which the Northern Virginia economy of the eighteenth century was dependent on forced labor. By the 1740s, one-third of the people in Fairfax County were enslaved Blacks. And many of the white residents were indentured servants to the few landholders in the county. Those who claimed ownership of people also controlled the county's power structure.

"It is safe to say that in 1749 Fairfax County was dominated by slave labor, that the majority of slaves were held in groups of over twenty slaves by the old established families and that the large slaveholders governed the county," wrote Donald Sweig in *Fairfax County, Virginia: A History*, published by the county's board of supervisors in 1978. "Further, much land and many of the slaves were held by men who lived outside of Fairfax County. It was a slave empire in the classic sense."[3]

The biggest of those slaveholders were the Fitzhugh family members who were granted parcels of Ravensworth upon William Fitzhugh's death in 1701. The process of subdividing those parcels would continue for more than three hundred years, until what was once Ravensworth became dotted with suburban homes on quarter-acre tracts. Today, Ravensworth survives only as the name of a shopping center and adjacent neighborhood.

By 1782, one of William Fitzhugh's descendants, also named William, enslaved 122 people at Ravensworth—nearly as many as the county's leading slaveholder, George Washington. Thomas Fitzhugh, another descendant, enslaved 91 people. By then, the enslaved population of the county had risen to 41 percent of the total, and the percentage of slaveholding white people had nearly doubled.[4]

Oak Hill

In 1790, Richard Fitzhugh, another descendant, built a house in the northern section of Ravensworth and called it Oak Hill. The home still stands today—after having gone through several renovation cycles—and remains privately owned.

It's a minor miracle Oak Hill wasn't razed in the development of this particular tract of suburbia in the early 1960s. Or that it didn't fall victim to abandonment, disrepair, and vandalism, like another Ravensworth mansion, Ossian Hall, which finally was burned in a fire department training exercise in 1959. Oak Hill managed to escape the wrecking ball and now stands as a testament to historic preservation. In 2004, Fairfax County entered into an unusual arrangement with Seville Homes, the developer that then controlled Oak Hill, under which the county paid $730,000 for an easement on the property. It limits the modifications owners can make to the house and grounds and requires them to open it to the public every year.

That was a significant development, because adding a site to the county's inventory of historic places does little to protect it. "You can name something an historical property up the ying-yang, but people can still develop it," says Sharon Bulova, who orchestrated the easement on Oak Hill when she served on the Fairfax County Board of Supervisors.[5] Bulova also organized a project to record the history of the county's Braddock District, in which Oak Hill is located, in the early 2000s.

By 2008, even after the historical easement was in place, Oak Hill had fallen into disrepair. It was eventually sold at auction and rehabilitated. Since then, a succession of owners have upheld the commitment to its preservation.

Still, more than two decades into the twenty-first century, celebrations of Oak Hill's history can be a bit awkward. Until recently, the annual Oak Hill History Days have tended to be festive affairs that focus heavily on the white experience—Thomas Jefferson slept here!—rather than on the lives of the people who were forced to work there in conditions that took an extreme physical toll.

In 2010, the Oak Hill History Day focused on the African American experience, with presentations on research into enslaved people and their experiences on the plantation. But their story hasn't attracted the attention paid to that of its white owners.

In a video produced in connection with a virtual Oak Hill celebration in 2020, James Walkinshaw, a representative on the board of supervisors whose district includes the plantation house, delivered a sobering message. "As we appreciate the architecture of the home, and the natural beauty of the site, we also acknowledge that human beings were held here in bondage," he said. Walkinshaw then read the names of forty-one enslaved people who were listed among the property of the plantation's owners in 1856:

Howard	Isabella
Augustin	Lucy
Charles	Herbert
Craven	Andrew
Richard	Berton
Griffin	Mary Ellen
Amanda	Jim
Julia	Sarah & child
Louisa	Polly
May	Lydia & child
Sarah & 4 children	Elizabeth
Hellen & 2 children	Henry
Spencer	Alice
Delphinia	Oscar
Henry	Johnson
Cornelia	Cora
Adaline	John
Molly	Peyton
Maria	William
Armistead	Alfred
Alice	

These people represented only a fraction of the enslaved at Fitzhugh properties. The absence of last names is not an indication that enslaved people didn't have them. White slaveholders and public officials simply refused to acknowledge their names, as if to drive home the point that the people held in bondage were less than fully human. So the enslaved kept their chosen last names hidden.[6]

Destruction

As a result, little official information is available in public records about African Americans in Fairfax County in the eighteenth and nineteenth centuries, despite the fact that regular slave auctions were held at the Fairfax Courthouse. Seeking details about the lives of the enslaved often leads one head-on into what historian John Browne, who has compiled a meticulously detailed history of the people and properties of Ravensworth, calls a "wall of unknowing."[7]

To the extent there are stories about the enslaved, generally "those impressions come through the eyes, ears, and pens of slave owners, committed to their own needs and beliefs in their superior humanity compared to those they held in bondage," writes Micki McElya in her study of the development of Arlington National Cemetery. "More often, the enslaved appear throughout the documents of plantation management, slave owning and generational wealth—inventories, insurance applications, invoices, wills—documents that list people as things and can only hint at the humanity of those enumerated within them."[8]

Because of this, the stories of African Americans who lived through enslavement tend to raise more questions than they answer. For example, in his 1982 memoir, Washington lawyer Edward Howrey, who bought the Oak Hill mansion and renovated it in 1935, included an anecdote involving "Aunt Lilly" Newman, who lived alone nearby and was almost one hundred years old.

"We called on Aunt Lilly one fine day and sat with her on the cabin porch," Howrey wrote. "Bent almost double with age, she rocked in her chair, sucked on her corncob pipe, and related the following tale in an old fashioned Negro dialect which I won't try to emulate."

Howrey then proceeds to engage in just such an act of imitation, writing that Newman warned them that a ghost that, according to local legend, haunted the property "gwine come back."[9]

Howrey's wife, Jane, was taken with the ghost story. According to notes from an interview with her in 1963, she said she dedicated both time and money in an attempt to convince Newman to tell the tale. "I have spent many afternoons and twenty 50 cent pieces trying to get her to talk," Howrey said. "She wanted to tell of the Lees." (Newman had worked at Ravensworth, which was owned by the family of Robert E. Lee's wife, Mary, who had briefly fled there at the onset of the Civil War.) "I wanted to hear of ghosts."[10]

Imagine the life Newman must have lived and the stories she could have told—and apparently wanted to tell, in addition to relating a ghost story. What was her life like on a plantation? What were her experiences as a child during the Civil War? How did she come into possession of a cabin in the woods?

According to Browne's research, an "Aunt Lillie" Gatewood married John Newman, who was born into slavery in about 1850 and eventually bought nine acres of land on what had been the Ravensworth plantation in 1886. They had eight known children. Today, there's an "Aunt Lilly Drive" in the Truro neighborhood between Oak Hill and Ilda. It's a short street and, somehow appropriately, a dead end.

When faced with the wall of unknowing, it's tempting to turn away and avoid facing what might lie behind it. But descendants of the enslaved, along with historians and researchers, are finding ways to chip away at the wall, bit by bit, until fuller stories of the marginalized emerge.

"We're recognizing that there is a much fuller history to tell," Walkinshaw says.[11]

"It's like opening a door to a new world," says Bulova. "There's a whole population that we haven't paid attention to. We haven't gathered that history like we should."[12]

"We're looking at these things in so many different ways, with more voices being brought in," says Maddy McCoy, who runs a public history consultancy in Alexandria, Virginia, and has done extensive research on the people who lived at Oak Hill and the surrounding community. "I'm going to be very frank: It's not just a bunch of white people anymore looking at things from a white lens."[13]

Crossroads

In seeking to understand the rise, decline, and remembrance of Ilda, it's crucial to realize how transportation networks have affected historical developments in the area. The site that became Ilda is centered on the intersection of two roads: Little River Turnpike running east and west, and Guinea Road running north and south.

These two roads are emblematic of a trend that would in large measure come to define the growth of Fairfax County over more than a century. As the county grew—steadily and then explosively in the mid-twentieth century—the demand for more and better roads was insatiable. And unlike in some other areas, including nearby counties, antidevelopment forces would have little success in stopping or even slowing the steady pace of new road construction and widening of existing thoroughfares. In the process, countless historical sites, including cemeteries, were paved over.

Little River Turnpike was not only critical to the development of Northern Virginia, but the financial model under which it was constructed at the turn of the eighteenth century presaged highway construction efforts hundreds of years later. Regional leaders came up with the idea of allowing private investors to raise capital to build the road and then collect tolls on the wagons and carriages that used it. In 1793, the Fairfax and Loudoun Turnpike Road Company took up the task of constructing what would become the third toll road in the United States. By 1806, it extended ten miles from Alexandria through what would become

Ilda to the town of Providence, which would later be renamed Fairfax City. Eventually the turnpike stretched all the way to its namesake Little River near Aldie, Virginia—a body of water of otherwise curiously little significance.

Not only did Little River Turnpike provide access to the Fairfax County Courthouse, in which all manner of legal and economic business needed to be conducted in person, it was critical for the movement and exchange of goods from rural areas to Alexandria, a major trade center and port.

Once Little River Turnpike was in operation, Fairfax County officials set about establishing connections to it via local roads. They began taking land via eminent domain and soon had their eyes on a piece of Fitzhugh-owned property that a commission determined in 1807 would provide "the most convenient way for a road from the Guinea Road . . . to fall in, or intersect the Little River Turnpike road."[14]

That's the earliest-known reference to the mysterious Guinea Road, although not because the road itself was new. A 1907 description of Fairfax County prepared by the board of supervisors describes it as one of the county's original "rolling roads," used to transport tobacco from fields in the center of the county to the Occoquan River.[15] In 1919, the *Fairfax Herald* described it as one of the oldest roads in the county (and also "the most neglected").[16] And against the Fitzhughs' objections, it was eventually extended to intersect with Little River Turnpike.

Why is it called Guinea Road? Over the years, local residents have offered various explanations. Some say it's because a guinea hen farm was located on the road.[17] An even less likely explanation is that it supposedly cost one guinea to traverse Little River Turnpike at the intersection with Guinea. (The nearest toll booth was in fact miles away in Annandale, and the road already had the name "Guinea" before it intersected with the turnpike.)[18]

Far more plausible is the explanation for why many places took on the name Guinea: it was a reference to the West African region from which millions of people were forcibly removed and enslaved. Everything from the Guinea Town settlement in New York's Hudson River Valley to the long list of countries around the world that incorporated Guinea into their names were connected in some way to western Africa—and ultimately the slave trade.

As early as the first few years of the nineteenth century, the name became associated with Virginia. William Byrd II, plantation owner, surveyor, and political leader of the Virginia Colony, noted the region's burgeoning population of enslaved African Americans and predicted that one day it would be called "New Guinea."[19]

That never formally happened, but the informal association with the name stuck. Historian John Chester Miller notes that when the importation of slaves was banned in 1807, Virginia enslavers went into the business of breeding slaves, and the state acquired a new nickname in the process: "Virginia had come to live in large measure by the export of its burgeoning slave population. Rapidly acquiring a reputation of the 'Guinea of the Union,' Virginia annually exported large numbers of surplus slaves, some of them bred deliberately for that purpose, to the newer regions of the south, especially the cotton fields of Mississippi and Alabama."[20]

In 1834, according to a 2015 *Smithsonian* article, the slave-trading firm Franklin & Armfield set out from Alexandria, Virginia (then a part of Fairfax County), with more than three hundred enslaved people chained together in what was known as a "coffle." They marched via the Little River Turnpike past what would become Ilda. They were forced to walk hundreds of miles to Tennessee, with some being sold along the way to cover the slave traders' expenses. Then they were likely put on flatboats for a journey farther south to Natchez, Mississippi.[21]

Not only is breeding human beings and tearing apart thousands of families to sell mothers, fathers, and children separately to far-away enslavers an almost unimaginably cruel development in the evolution of the slavery economy, it is among many pieces of evidence that "Guinea" was a common usage of the time to describe western Africa and the people who were sold into slavery there. A farm owned by Thomas Jefferson was called "Guinea." Settlements of free African Americans were sometimes called "New Guinea."[22]

Oral tradition, along with historical records and archaeological evidence, indicates that enslaved Black people lived and died in the areas adjacent to Guinea Road. They certainly were buried there. And unlike, for example, the community of Guinea in Gloucester County, Virginia, "Guinea" was neither similar to a family name in the area nor a prominent regional reference. It seems much more likely that the road got its name because of the people who were forced to live near there than that the moniker derives from hen farms, toll fees, or some other source.

Whatever the origin of its name, Guinea Road, at its intersection with Little River Turnpike, was where Ilda would be built, and the junction would become a place of intermittent controversy and conflict thereafter. Especially the plot of land on the southwest corner of the intersection on which sat a small cemetery.

"No Mean Action"

In 1807, William Gooding Jr. opened a namesake tavern on the brand-new Little River Turnpike. His father was a tenant on a parcel of land controlled by a man who had in turn leased it from Henry Fitzhugh. Gooding's Tavern soon became a popular landmark on the turnpike, known for its owner's hospitality, fried chicken, peaches and honey, and "Cornwallis," a corn whiskey.

As the business grew, William Gooding started buying up Ravensworth land. In 1814, he purchased sixty acres north of the turnpike, where the tavern and his home were located. He later bought another one hundred acres south of the road. His operation later grew to include a blacksmith shop and stable. At the time of his death in 1861, the *Alexandria Gazette* declared that Gooding "was, in many respects, a remarkable man. Without education, by his honest industry he amassed a comfortable independence, without ever stooping to mean action."

William Gooding's will lists among his property thirty-one enslaved people, whom he doled out to his children, along with "the future increase of the females among them."

Gooding's sons, Peter and William H. Gooding, eventually became major landowners, slaveholders, and influential local leaders themselves. Today, the centerpiece of the Goodings' land is a bucolic sliver of suburbia, home to the Pleasant Valley Memorial Park and the Little River United Church of Christ. The cemetery was established in 1963 by a small group of developers who wanted to create a last resting place for people of all backgrounds and faiths.[23] Strolling along the small road that winds into the woods between the church and the cemetery, it doesn't take much imagination to picture what it must have looked like in the mid-nineteenth century.

Of course, keep walking and soon modernity introduces cognitive dissonance into the scene. Against a backdrop of a tract of houses on one side and an electrical substation on the other sits the Gooding family's small cemetery. The graveyard is fairly well-preserved, although it's easy to trip over some of the smaller headstones in the tall grass.

In 1958, Mabel Lowry, a descendant of William Gooding, reported to her daughter-in-law that there were some "colored graves" to the north of the Gooding family cemetery and that she had located stones there in 1952.[24] A county map of the area also issued in 1958 shows the presence of grave markers in that area. Today, the area immediately to the north of the Gooding plots is overgrown and strewn with trash. But several of what appear to be fieldstone markers are visible in the underbrush.

As for the Gooding headstones, many of their inscriptions are worn away, but some are still legible, after brushing aside the two-foot-tall clumps of grass that cover them. "Sacred to the memory of Peter Gooding," one reads. "A kind neighbor and a friend to the poor."

At the time of his death, Peter Gooding held twenty-seven people in bondage.

Scavenged and Ravaged

As the Goodings and others bought more land and held more enslaved people, the increasingly strained connection between the northern and southern portions of the country ruptured over the issue of the expansion of slavery. The Civil War would upend economic systems, social arrangements, and even the physical landscape of Fairfax County.

Northern Virginia was in a unique position during the war. Virginia as a whole was the heart and soul of the Confederacy and the site of several of the war's most monumental battles. But while only one major engagement, the Battle of Chantilly, was fought within Fairfax County, the area was a place of constantly shifting battle lines and repeated devastation as both sides moved troops and munitions, dug earthworks, and sent out foraging parties.

There was a constant flow of military traffic on the Little River Turnpike, and troops routinely scavenged the countryside for supplies. At the outset of the war, Union troops took control of the city of Alexandria and extensively used the roads connecting the surrounding areas to the key port city.

Skirmishes were frequent, including several in and around what would become Ilda. On November 5, 1861, for example, Pvt. Edward S. E. Newbury and Cpl. Thomas Edwards of the Third Infantry Regiment of the New Jersey Volunteers went on a scouting mission to the Oak Hill plantation house. They'd heard that a group of Confederates were gathering at the home, whose then owner, David Fitzhugh, had fled the property due to its precarious location in no-man's-land.

Newbury and Edwards made their way to the house, where they encountered an enslaved Black woman who was tending to her ill son. From her, they learned that Fitzhugh was expected to return that evening. The two men hid in the house's detached kitchen and, as night fell, found themselves in a firefight. Edwards was shot in the back, and he and Newbury fled to a nearby cornfield. They hid out until 4:00 a.m. Then Newbury hoisted Edwards onto his back and began a long trek back to their camp in Alexandria, where they arrived around 7:00 p.m.[25]

But what of the enslaved woman who had helped them? Her name, that of her ailing son, and the story of how they came to find themselves alone at a plantation house in a hotly contested region during the early days of the Civil War weren't considered significant enough to record in various reports of the incident.

More unsettling and deadly than the intermittent skirmishes were the daring raids of John S. Mosby and his Confederate rangers. They continued on and off throughout the course of the war, including one in September 1863 that took place near Gooding's Tavern. Mosby and his men came upon a Union contingent of fifty soldiers moving more than one hundred horses. Mosby's report on the action gives a sense of the horror, confusion and, undoubtedly, property damage that ensued:

My men went at them with a yell that terrified the Yankees and scattered them in all directions. A few taking shelter under cover of the houses, opened fire on us. They were soon silenced, however. At the very moment when I had succeeded in routing them, I was compelled to retire from the fight, having been shot through the side and thigh.... Over 100 horses came into our possession, though a good many were lost in bringing them out at night; also 12 prisoners, arms, etc. I learn that 6 of the enemy were killed. In this affair my loss was 2 killed and 3 wounded.[26]

The back-and-forth of Union and Confederate troops took its toll, especially on local civilians whose crops and livestock were frequently seized to supply armies. Their lands also were sometimes stripped of trees used to build fortifications. "What can be described as a cruel war of attrition was waged by soldiers on the unfortunate civilian inhabitants of Fairfax County's no-man's-land and its occupied farms and towns," reads a 2002 county inventory of Civil War sites. "By the war's end, Fairfax County's antebellum rebound had been negated; the county was left agriculturally devastated with its infrastructure mostly destroyed."[27]

John Trowbridge of Massachusetts, who toured the South to report on conditions in the immediate postwar period, painted a bleak picture of the county. It showed "no sign of human industry," he reported, "save here and there a sickly, half-cultivated corn field. The country for the most part consisted of fenceless fields abandoned to weeds, stump lots and undergrowth."[28]

But out of the ruination of the war some saw a promise of a brighter future. Relatively cheap land, a mild climate, and the proximity of Washington, D.C., made the county attractive to northerners looking for a new start and to formerly enslaved people seeking their own farms to work and businesses to run.[29]

After Peter Gooding died just before the outbreak of the war, his son Peter Jr. inherited parcels of land in the vicinity of Little River Turnpike and Guinea Road. It was a war-torn region, changed physically, politically, and sociologically by the Confederacy's defeat. As newcomers moved in, families like the Goodings decided to sell off their land piece by piece. All they needed were ready buyers.

Enter Horace Gibson and Moses Parker.

2

Reconstruction

IF THE INTERSECTION OF Little River Turnpike and Guinea Road is today typical of suburbia, the environs of the city of Fairfax just a few miles to the west are its quintessence. The area in and around where the turnpike converges with US 50 is a free-for-all of development. Until very recently it was still dotted with old-time roadside motels of the kind that a traveling salesman would have frequented in the 1950s: the Breezeway, the Hy-Way, and the Lee-High Inn (with its delightful, if oddly themed, nautical architecture). In between are a grab bag of contemporary chain stores and restaurants: Party City, Planet Fitness, Mattress Warehouse, 7-Eleven, Starbucks (and Dunkin'), McDonald's (and Burger King), and many, many more.

Pull into the parking lot of one particular retail strip, and a few steps away sits a small expanse of green next to the site of a huge apartment complex that was under construction on a summer's day in 2021. Heavy equipment roared and sputtered in the heavy, humid air, as if literally trying to pull the complex from the earth to feed the ever-burgeoning appetite for housing in the Fairfax area.

In this small plot of greenery, almost swallowed up by the apartment project and other nearby development, someone, presumably without any other place to call home, had pitched a tent. Its bright-yellow color stood out among the vegetation, and its modesty as a form of shelter contrasted starkly with the nearby residential buildings and businesses. The tent was a literally glaring reminder that not all Fairfax County residents share in the prosperity of living in one of the richest counties in the nation.

The one-acre area surrounding where the tent stood is hallowed ground: Jermantown Cemetery, established in 1868 to provide a final resting place for African Americans in the area. Many of the people laid to rest in Jermantown Cemetery were noteworthy Black residents in Fairfax County in the late nineteenth and early twentieth centuries. Even those who had worked in support of the Confederate cause were not exempt from burial in the segregated cemetery. George Lamb, a free African American who worked as a personal attendant to Capt. William H. Dulany of the Confederacy's Seventeenth Virginia Infantry (known as the "Fairfax Rifles") is interred there. Almost one hundred years after his death, Lamb endured the indignity of being used to push the spurious claim that thousands of African Americans had taken up arms against the Union and fought for the Confederacy. He was a servant, not a soldier.[1]

One of the many gravestones in Jermantown Cemetery stands out. It marks the burial plot of Horace Gibson and his wife, Margaret. "Peace be Thine," reads its inscription.

That's a relatively common epitaph on gravestones. But it seems a particularly apt phrase to grace the burial plots of Horace and Margaret, because peace was hard to come by for them, especially Horace, during their life on Earth. He would not only be involved in multiple legal disputes but would endure savage physical attacks. This makes it all the more impressive that the Gibsons enjoyed the success that they did—professionally, economically, and culturally. Their place in Jermantown Cemetery indicates the prominence they gained in Fairfax County. But it also is a marker of the fact that they would always be separate, apart, and on unequal footing with the white residents of the county.

Horace Gibson was born into slavery on April 15, 1817, in Culpeper County, Virginia. According to records referred to by Gibson family members and family oral tradition, his parents were Jonathan C. Gibson, a white slaveholder, and Sarah Anna, an enslaved African American.[2] There are no records of exactly when Horace married Margaret, who also was enslaved. Indeed, records are scant for any part of this period of Horace Gibson's and Moses Parker's lives. But their families' oral traditions about their lives are rich and detailed.

Tapping into such traditions is critical to telling stories like that of Ilda and its founders, because it provides a way to give voice to those who are largely absent from official records and history books.

Maddy McCoy conducted extensive research on the African American experience in Fairfax County early in her career. She got her start as a researcher on an official investigation into Ilda's history at the City of Fairfax Regional Library. Much of the information available about the enclave stems from the families' oral traditions, she notes. That information is often treated skeptically by historians and discounted if it can't be confirmed by official records that contain little information about the African American experience. Especially in official government analyses and proceedings, McCoy says, "oral history means jack if you don't have documentation—which is a huge part of this discrimination."[3]

In the case of the Gibson and Parker families, some of the history that has been carried down through oral tradition has been documented. Other parts remain unverifiable. But it is not a fable. Much of the information that has been passed on to their descendants is supported not only by official records but by interviews and documentation preserved by family members. Their work has been supplemented by exhaustive research by not only their descendants but historians, archivists, and archaeologists.

According to the family's oral tradition, Gibson was trained as a blacksmith and often was hired out to other white landowners in and around Culpeper. For an enslaved person, this was at least a somewhat fortuitous situation, because it afforded Gibson the opportunity to put away money to purchase his freedom. What's more, it gave him the opportunity to establish a postwar business. Many of the formerly enslaved after the Civil War had little choice but to go back to work for their former enslavers as low-paid (or, in some cases, unpaid) laborers.

In the early 1860s, Gibson was able to purchase his freedom and move his family to Fairfax County. According to his descendants, entries in a family Bible indicate he and Margaret eventually had twelve children: Strother, Adalina, Wesley, Matilda, Brook E., Mary, John Edward, George H., Emily, Lewis, Henry, and Tommie. Henry and Tommie died as infants.

Property records of this era don't indicate where the family lived, but according to oral tradition, they took up residence in a shantytown along Guinea Road near Little River Turnpike that had long been home to enslaved people.[4] Little is known of this wartime period in the Gibsons' life—exactly where they lived, how Horace made a living, and how they navigated the vicissitudes of war in the county.

Limited Freedom

Whatever the Gibsons' specific situation, winning freedom from an enslaved life during the Civil War hardly led to a comfortable existence. Under Virginia law, any African American in the state was presumed to be a slave. It was the responsibility of free

African Americans to carry papers at all times providing proof of their status.

All efforts to challenge that principle on the grounds that it conflicted with the founding ideals of the United States were quickly quashed. In a 1913 dissertation, John Henderson Russell wrote, "In 1806, George Wythe, chancellor of the state of Virginia, gave as grounds for decreeing the freedom of three persons claimed as slaves that freedom is the birthright of every human being. He laid it down as a general proposition that whenever one person claims to hold another in slavery, the onus probandi lies on the claimant. This application of the Declaration of Independence was completely repudiated by the supreme court of appeals when the case came up for final review."[5] One of the judges in that review offered the following hypothetical in the decision: "Three persons, a black or mulatto man or woman with a flat nose and wooly head; a copper-colored with long jetty black or straight hair; and one with a fair complexion, brown hair, not woolly, nor inclined thereto, with a prominent Roman nose, were brought together before a judge upon a suit of habeas corpus. . . . How must the judge act in this case? . . . He must deliver the [white person and Native American] out of custody, and permit the negro to remain in slavery, until he could produce proof of his freedom."[6]

The "freedom" the judge spoke of was, for Black Virginians not enslaved, altogether different from that enjoyed by white Virginia residents—and in fact became more restrictive during the first century of American history. In the colonial era, there was little regulation of the movements of free African Americans. But once their numbers reached several thousand people, officials imposed escalating restrictions. In 1793, free African Americans were prohibited from entering Virginia from another state to take up residence unless they were employed as a servant to a white person. Those already in the state couldn't go to another county from the one they were registered in without a copy of the registration—requiring a trip to the courthouse. After 1848, they couldn't travel to a state that prohibited slavery and return to Virginia.[7]

Even if free African Americans managed to keep and hold papers verifying their freedom—and those papers were accepted by any authority figure they came into contact with—they were explicitly unwelcome in the state. Any slave freed after 1806 had to petition the court of the county in which they lived for permission to remain in the state for more than a year.

In Fairfax County, such petitions initially were routinely granted to formerly enslaved people deemed worthy of remaining in the jurisdiction, and often the requirement was simply not acknowledged at all. "In fact, the laws respecting the free blacks were not enforced in Fairfax County," a group of county historians declared in 1977. The "law requiring the registration of all free blacks and re-registration every three years was largely ignored. Many free blacks lived in Fairfax for five, ten, even twenty years without bothering to register. The registrations were allowed to lapse for five, six, or any other number of years. Such laxity in enforcement of the law suggests that the free Blacks were an accepted, perhaps even valued, segment of antebellum Fairfax society."[8]

Accepted, perhaps. And maybe in some cases valued, although not as equals. But the laws were on the books, and the threat of enforcement, not to mention extralegal actions against free African Americans, always loomed.

In 1855, for example, a man named Lewis Casey, who had been recently freed from enslavement, sought to put down roots in Fairfax County. The justices of the county court refused his petition, even though they found him to be "honest, sober and industrious." The problem, they said, was that it would simply be "impolitic to encourage any larger increase in this class of our population."[9]

The irony was that the Black population of Fairfax County was actually falling at the time. It dropped 3 percent from 1840 to 1860. The key factor in the decline was a decrease in the number of enslaved people. From 1840 to 1860, the enslaved population dropped nearly 10 percent, from 3,453 to 3,116. The biggest driver of the shift was an increase in the sale of enslaved people, the result of a depressed agricultural economy.[10]

At the same time, the population of free African Americans in the county was heading in the opposite direction, increasing by 50 percent. But their numbers remained small, growing from 448 to 672. And even for free Black residents of Virginia, inequities abounded. Taxation was one example. In 1850, a tax of one dollar annually was levied on all free African Americans between the ages of twenty-one and fifty-five in Virginia. Ten years later, another tax on free persons, both white and Black, was levied. When it came time to determine which one of the two should be collected from African Americans, the answer came down from the state: both.[11]

When the Civil War ended, Fairfax County was no longer in no-man's-land militarily. But its residents, new and old, could feel the ground shifting beneath their feet. For starters, the demographics of the county were rapidly changing. Northerners had already started to move in before the war. By 1847, two hundred northern families had relocated to Fairfax County. Three years later, one out of every three adult males living in the county had come from a northern state or out of the country. Many were farmers but cultivated their land themselves rather than by using an enslaved workforce. Some, like the Quakers, hoped to demonstrate that an agricultural economy could be sustained without the use of slave labor.[12]

Northern abolitionists actively supported this movement. For example, Eli Thayer, an ally of John Brown, "sponsored the immigration of Northern farmers into Virginia, confident that free-labor competition would soon rout slavery," writes Ira Berlin in his seminal work on free African Americans in the South before the Civil War, *Slaves without Masters*.[13]

Other northern newcomers didn't share a zeal for the abolition of slavery. But they did bring with them new agricultural techniques. Before the war, extensive farming and the lack of a staple crop led to an agricultural depression. Residents eked out a living from what crops they could grow, through fishing and via the sale of enslaved people.

Then the northern immigrants brought a revolution in cultivation—in the form of manure.

In 1842, one of the Quakers, Jacob Haight of New York's Hudson River Valley, bought a 750-acre estate known as Sully in Fairfax County and began using it to demonstrate modern farming techniques—specifically, the application of sheep manure and bird guano as fertilizers. (He also relied on other emerging practices like crop rotation.) Soon, these and commercial fertilizers were being liberally applied to farmland across the county. As a result, the quantity and quality of crops increased dramatically.[14]

This, in turn, lifted the economic tide and created new opportunities for skilled workers that only increased after the war. Among the occupations in demand was blacksmith.

New Arrivals

About nine miles east of Jermantown Cemetery sits the Second Baptist Church of Falls Church, a prominent African American place of worship founded shortly after the Civil War. Behind the church is a cemetery, larger than Jermantown and better tended. On a cold, blustery midwinter's day in 2022, it was quiet other than the occasional rush of wind. Majestic cedar trees dotted the landscape, each with at least one small headstone visible at its base.

The cemetery is surrounded by houses, an apartment complex, and the athletic fields of the James Lee Community Center. "Home of the Razorbacks" reads the scoreboard on a football field abutting the graveyard to the south. Some of the graves hug the property lines tightly.

The cemetery contains a mix of graves dating from the nineteenth century to the present day. Dirt from a pair of freshly dug graves is piled in the rear. Memorials have been left on various gravesites—flowers, solar-powered lights, a basketball. At 3:00 p.m. sharp, bells ring out from another church off in the distance, playing "Faith of Our Fathers." In the Parker family section of the cemetery, almost all of the inscriptions are worn away. One, reading "To the Memory of Sarah E. Parker," is visible. She died as a one-year-old child in 1887.

In the row in front of Sarah's marker stands another in which the "Parker" name can be made out. Is that an "M" at the top? Records indicate that Moses Parker is buried here. But it's fitting that exactly where he lies is something of mystery, just as Moses himself was.

If relatively little is known about Horace Gibson's early life and his experiences shortly after purchasing the limited freedom African Americans were allowed, still less is available in the form of documentary evidence about Moses Parker. According to family records and oral history, Parker was born into slavery in 1825 in Culpeper County, bearing the name of his "owner," Jonathan Parker.

If both Parker and Gibson shared the names of their enslavers, that would have been unusual. It has long been commonly assumed that slaveholders attached their last names to those they enslaved, especially if they had fathered them. But McCoy has determined that in Fairfax County at least, that was rarely the case. In her research in the county, she unearthed data that enabled her to connect naming patterns and family relationships in a way that had never been done before. She was able to determine the first and last names of many enslaved people and discovered that only 5 percent of them shared a last name with their slaveholder.[15]

Parker married Emily Taylor, who was born in 1832. They had nine children: Julia Ann, Page, Mildred, Moses Jr., Melinda, Major Stanfield, Robert, James H., and Mary Louisa.[16]

According to family lore, Parker, like Gibson, was trained as a blacksmith. He and Emily moved to Fairfax County around 1865, settling in the same area as the Gibsons. Family tradition also holds that this was no coincidence, that Gibson and Parker knew each other in Culpeper County before journeying to Fairfax. The two did share a history that seems more than coincidental: both were trained as blacksmiths and were held in bondage in the same general area.

Nevertheless, one family historian acknowledged that "I cannot offer any concrete proof, only oral history and notes passed down through the family," for the assertion that Gibson and Parker were acquainted before they arrived in Fairfax County.[17] Whether or not they knew each other before they took up residence in the county, their lives would quickly become intertwined in both personal and professional ways.

The Parkers did not arrive in Fairfax County alone. They were joined by a man named Robert Williams, a somewhat enigmatic figure. He, like Horace Gibson and Moses Parker, would become a landowner in the Ilda area, right next to the Parkers and close to the Gibsons. Williams is listed in the 1870 federal census as a member of Moses's household, and he identified his occupation as "cook on a schooner."[18] He reported that he had one hundred dollars in personal property. Williams listed no real estate, though he had recently purchased land.[19]

Apparently, Williams, who never married, ultimately came to be treated as a family member by the Parker and Gibson clans.

In his will, Williams made clear his close connections to the families:

> I give and bequeath to James H. Parker (son of Emily Parker) all of my property in Fairfax County Virginia consisting of house and two acres of land more or less, lying on the Little River Turnpike and bounded by said turnpike—the farm owned by Henry Sewell and the farm owned by the late Moses Parker. And also to the said James H. Parker, all of my household furniture and personal effects and debts due me, to dispose of as he may think proper. Provided however that all of these bequests shall be subject to the payment of a just compensation to Margaret Gibson for her attention and car[e] to me personally during my disability.[20]

Swindlers and Suits

It's clear that Horace Gibson had accumulated some savings by the time the Civil War ended. Because on November 8, 1865, when a man named George Oliver rode into the Little River Turnpike–Guinea Road area with another horse in tow, looking for a customer, he found one in Gibson. They struck a deal, and Gibson paid Oliver fifty dollars.[21]

There was just one problem: the animal wasn't Oliver's. He was a horse thief.

Oliver made off for Washington, D.C., with his ill-gotten gains, but the law eventually caught up with him. On December 11, he was arrested.

But Oliver's arrest left Gibson in trouble, too. "The sheriff afterward took the [horse] from Gibson as a mare stolen from a man in Loudoun County, Va.," the *Alexandria Gazette* reported.[22] That man was Sheridan Palmer, and he wasn't taking the theft of his horse lightly. He sued Gibson, who ended up having to pay him a rather hefty sum: seventy-five dollars to cover the value of the horse and Palmer's other expenses.

And that wasn't all. According to a later court filing, Gibson contended he "was put to other great . . . expenses, and expended a great amount of time, to wit, the expense of forty dollars and the time of thirty days in and about defending the title to the said horse, and in and about defending [Palmer's] suit."[23]

Gibson fought back in the American way: by filing a lawsuit himself, against Oliver. That might have seemed like a fool's errand for a formerly enslaved person. But even before the end of the Civil War, free African Americans in Northern Virginia exercised their right to take their grievances before the courts. And they had a surprising amount of success.[24]

So, in a written filing on a fragile piece of paper buried deep in the files at the Fairfax County Circuit Court Historic Records Office, the court duly noted in March 1866 that "Horace Gibson complains of George Oliver, who . . . on the 8th day of November 1865 at the county of Fairfax by his false fraudulent and deceitful representations of to the said plaintiff that a certain horse that the defendant has in his possession was really his property and that he had good right to sell the same, induced the said plaintiff to buy the said horse from the said defendant and to pay the said defendant the sum of fifty dollars whereas in truth and in fact the said horse was not the property of the said defendant at that time, nor ever was."

"We the jury find for the plaintiff," reads the almost completely faded handwriting on another piece of what looks like scrap paper but is an official court record. Oliver was ordered to pay Gibson seventy-five dollars.[25]

Property Owners

At the end of his legal odyssey, Gibson still had saved enough money to achieve what must have seemed impossible to him just a few years earlier: becoming a landowner. In March 1868, he paid Peter Gooding Jr. $150 for five acres of land on the north side of Little River Turnpike at its intersection with Guinea Road.

"Horace's earnings as a blacksmith, possibly supplemented by his award from the 1867 lawsuit, most likely enabled him to purchase the land," reads a detailed report on the Gibson-Parker experience prepared in connection with an investigation into the history of the Guinea Road Cemetery. "By the time Gibson moved to the area, William H. Gooding was the most senior member of his family left. He had continued running his father's tavern (hotel) during the Civil War, but by 1865, the tavern and the businesses that went with it were gone."

"It is interesting that Gibson purchased land only a short distance west of the location where the Goodings had run a tavern and blacksmith's shop for decades," the report continues.[26]

It is indeed interesting, and perhaps not coincidental. County tax records from 1869 list Gibson as living at "W H Goodings." (Records covering 1866 to 1868 don't indicate a place of residence.)[27] He may have learned from the Goodings or realized on his own that by shuttering their businesses, they were opening an opportunity for other trained blacksmiths. As fate—or perhaps foresighted planning—would have it, there were two such people in the immediate area.

The deed to Gibson's property indicates that before the purchase was complete, he had already begun construction of two buildings on the site: a house and a blacksmith shop. And Gibson was beginning to amass a degree of wealth. For county tax purposes in 1867, he listed two horses valued at $100 among his possessions, along with two hogs ($10), one carriage ($40), and pieces of furniture worth a total of $50.

In 1868, Gibson still owned the horses, hogs, and furniture at the same values as the year before, but the carriage he listed among his belongings was now valued at $50. Before he officially owned land, his work was clearly paying off. And afterward, success seemed to come quickly. In 1870, Gibson's taxable possessions included two horses ($100), one head of cattle ($10), five hogs ($25), two carriages ($35), various mechanic's tools ($10), and farming implements ($15).[28]

The blacksmith shop would grow to become a fixture of the community, the centerpiece of Ilda, and a landmark in that part of Fairfax County. Road descriptions, deeds, court records, and other documents spanning decades use "Horace Gibson's Shop" as a reference point. Maps are marked with "Blacksmith Shop" or simply "B.S.S."

The shop was a success from the beginning, due in part to two central factors: it catered to all races and economic classes, and it was strategically located. Gibson "served everybody—black, white, poor, and rich," his great-great-grandson would later say. "And the Little River Turnpike was a good location because the Fairfax County Courthouse was the seat of the judicial system, and also it was the county seat, where people came and took care of their legislative business. . . . They would use the Little River Turnpike to come back and forth from Alexandria and Arlington, which were more developed than that part of Fairfax County, to go to see the judge or go to see the legislators."[29]

Indeed, the primary mode of transportation on Little River Turnpike was the horse-drawn carriage, which carried with it the need not only to regularly board and reshoe horses but to repair the vehicles worn down by travel on the rough road. Then there were the local farmers, who regularly needed their implements sharpened or repaired.[30]

Until the post–Civil War era, Guinea Road ended at its intersection with the turnpike. But with the opening of the blacksmith shop and the subsequent growth of Ilda, it became a crossroads. Gibson and his neighbors carved a country road from the shop

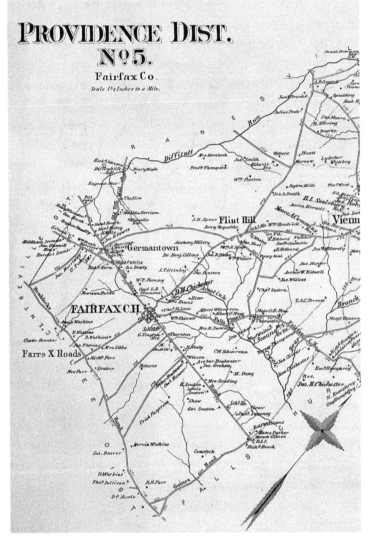

This detail from an 1878 Fairfax County map shows Horace Gibson and Moses Parker (on lower right edge) among major landholders. (Courtesy of the Fairfax County Public Library)

to a point in Merrifield, where it intersected with a road running from Fairfax Court House to Falls Church.[31]

At the time, local residents were responsible for the upkeep of such roads. In 1878, Gibson was excused from such duty "on account of physical disability."[32] That was not because he was trying to shirk the chore of road maintenance. In fact, not only was he surely in a physical condition that would have left him unable to work on road construction, it was a wonder he was alive. On the night of September 10, 1877, Gibson had been viciously assaulted at the shop by five drunk men—three Black and two white. The men showed up at the shop, and according to a newspaper account, "commenced to upset the vehicles there and act in a very disorderly manner. Gibson remonstrated with them, when they set upon him and beat him terribly, mashing his face almost to a jelly." The men finally ran off and were later arrested. Gibson managed to get to a doctor and have his wounds treated.[33]

Eventually the road fell into disuse, and in 1907 local residents petitioned to have it discontinued. Reviewers of the application concluded, "There is no travel on this road except that done by parties having property abutting thereon. The road is in very poor condition and it would take a large amount of money to make it passable." Nevertheless, the road remained in existence for at least another twenty-two years. In 1929, a county-appointed committee determined that it was not an official road and hadn't been maintained by the county.[34]

But the road set an important precedent. Decades later, a street running roughly parallel to the old road would be built from Merrifield toward Ilda, eventually connecting to Little River Turnpike in Ilda. But its location about a quarter mile from the Guinea Road intersection would contribute to vexing traffic issues in the area—issues that would put Guinea Road and Ilda in local headlines again in the twenty-first century.

A prime location may not have been the only factor in the success of the blacksmith shop. In an oral history interview conducted in 1975, Francis Honesty, a lifelong Fairfax resident, noted that in the postwar period, sawmills did a brisk business producing railroad ties. As a result, "blacksmithing evolved as a popular trade among the freedmen below Fairfax, for the saw millers often needed worn equipment and broken bolts . . . replaced."[35]

Whatever combination of factors led to its success, business was brisk at the shop. Over the next two decades, Gibson would accumulate additional property near the blacksmith operation. In 1871 he bought a tract of land from A. D. Osgood that had been previously held by Peter and Margarette Gooding. The next year he added another three acres adjacent to the property he already owned.

In 1884, Gibson purchased twenty-one acres from Elizabeth Fitzhugh and other heirs of William Fitzhugh. It was on the opposite side of Little River Turnpike from the shop and down Guinea Road a short distance. He would add further parcels in the Ilda vicinity in the years to come.

By this time, Gibson owned a great deal of the real estate in what was developing into a small but important community. At the time of his death in 1912, he had built up an estate valued at more than $1,400.[36] Considering that he had been enslaved until nearly the end of the Civil War, had arrived in the county without a job or a place to live, and started a business from scratch as an African American in the heart of the Confederacy, he was a stunning success.

Partners

Gibson wasn't alone in achieving his accomplishments. Even if he and Moses Parker hadn't already known each other before moving to Fairfax County, they certainly were acquainted by the late 1860s. That's when they became neighbors and partners.

According to local tax records, Parker had been in the county since at least 1866. That year, he listed among his personal property two horses worth $40, one head of cattle ($20), four hogs ($20), and another $20 worth of furniture. In 1867, Parker still had two horses (this time valued at a total of $50), two head of cattle, four hogs, and $50 in furniture. By 1868, he retained a pair of horses, but now they were valued at $150. The cattle, hogs, and furniture remained in his possession. Like Gibson, he clearly was beginning to make a comfortable living.[37]

Gibson and Parker were established citizens of Fairfax County by 1867. Both voted in the election that year on whether to hold a constitutional convention in Virginia as part of the process of readmission to the Union. Voting records show they participated in the election two years later as well.[38]

By 1870, about 120 African Americans owned significant amounts of land in Fairfax County. Seventeen percent of people freed from enslavement were living on land they had purchased.[39] A year earlier, Moses Parker had joined this group.

In 1869, Parker and Robert Williams paid Peter Gooding Jr. $84 for six acres of land on Little River Turnpike, just west of Guinea Road and adjacent to Gibson's land. According to the deed, Parker and Williams were already living on the land at the time of the purchase. (Four years later, they would legally divide it between them.) By 1878, their homes and the blacksmith shop appeared on a map of the area. In the intervening years, the shop would become the heart of Ilda and its central business.

The Gibson-Parker partnership in laying the foundation for a racially mixed community was unusual. Most African Americans in the post–Civil War period congregated together by choice or necessity. After emancipation, many formerly enslaved people in Fairfax County stayed on or near the land they had been forced to work. Others moved out, either to Washington, D.C., or northern states. Few moved into the Fairfax area and stayed. Those who did usually lived in segregated communities.

Even before the war, there were enclaves of free African Americans in Fairfax County. One of the most prominent and successful was Gum Springs, near Mount Vernon. It was founded in 1833 by West Ford, who grew up enslaved by George Washington's family and was freed when he turned twenty-one.

Gum Springs became a haven both for slaves who had been freed and those who had escaped a life of bondage by running away. It was, not surprisingly, hardly an earthly paradise: its muddy soil wasn't really suitable for successful farming, it lacked paved roads for decades, and housing was perpetually substandard. Yet its residents forged a community that lasts to this day.[40]

Gum Springs was, by the standards of Black communities, a success story. But racist policies and practices not only hindered its early development and were reinforced during the Jim Crow era but have continued into the twentieth and twenty-first centuries. Most of Gum Springs' residents worked on farms in the surrounding areas in the late nineteenth century and struggled to earn their way into the middle class.

In 1961, local officials ordered residents to demolish homes dismissed as shanties, forcing them to form their own housing development corporation to build new homes. Forty years later, the struggle continued as residents took to the streets to protest a plan to widen a highway running through the community that they said would make the neighborhood dangerous for pedestrians and cyclists.[41]

After the war, more than a dozen African American communities sprung up in Fairfax County. One of the most prominent was Mills Crossroads, located about three and a half miles from the blacksmith shop. Both Black and white families settled in Mills Crossroads during Reconstruction. The area was attractive to formerly enslaved African Americans and Union war veterans because of the availability of cheap farmland.[42] The village is prominently marked on an 1878 map of the region. Eventually, it took on the name Merrifield, after a prominent local white resident.

From the start, Merrifield was a divided community. And it stayed that way. A descendant of Horace Gibson who grew up nearby in the 1950s remembered that a road cutting through the heart of the community served as a line of demarcation. "Gallows Road was a dividing line between blacks and whites," he said. "Blacks were on the east side of Gallows Road. Whites were on the west side."[43]

Other African American communities sprang up in post–Civil War Fairfax County in the towns of Herndon, Vienna, Falls Church, and Chantilly. They were mostly made up of formerly enslaved people who had been denied the opportunity to learn a skill or trade. That meant they had little choice but to hire themselves out as farm laborers, sometimes to the same people who had enslaved them.

There were smaller mixed-race communities that until recently were lost to history. Near the Oak Hill house on the old Ravensworth plantation, for example, a small enclave sprang up with the division of the plantation among the Fitzhugh relatives starting before the Civil War and continuing afterward. Three African Americans who had been enslaved at Oak Hill—John H. Newman, Oscar Newman, and Richard P. Newman—bought parcels of land near the house. Other settlers joined them.

In the early 2000s, Maddy McCoy and other researchers discovered an unnamed African American cemetery in the Oak Hill community. The enclave had so faded from memory that local historians were unaware of its existence. Oak Hill was a farming community lacking the strategic location that Ilda had, and for its Black residents, the lack of a nearby school eventually made living there untenable.

As Black citizens put down roots in Fairfax County, their numbers began to grow. Between 1860 and 1870, the Black population of the county increased by 13 percent. The following decade, it went up another 23 percent. By that time, more than five thousand African Americans were living in the county.[44]

This reflected the reality that the demographics of the entire state of Virginia were changing. Realistic politicians acknowledged the situation. In 1874, then governor James L. Kemper delivered an address to the Virginia Assembly in which he took up the subject of relations between the races. Kemper was no radical. He had been staunchly pro-slavery before the Civil War and served as a general in the Confederate army, seeing action in numerous major battles, including Gettysburg, where he was injured.

Still, with the war over and Reconstruction in full swing, Kemper stated what sounds obvious in retrospect. "We must all enjoy a common prosperity, or we must all go down in a common ruin," he said. "Each race [must] stand up for the interests and rights of the other and of both."[45]

The conservative editors of the *Fairfax News* excoriated Kemper's speech. "We do not believe one word of it," they wrote. What they did believe was that "the negro is wholly dependent upon the white race for his prosperity as he now enjoys it, [but] the white race is in no degree, or sense, dependent upon the colored race for a like condition. In short, we think the two races would be infinitely better off if they were separated by an impassable gulf. The Anglo-Saxon's career is onward and upward, regardless of what the colored race may do."

The first enslaved people arrived in Virginia in 1619. For more than two hundred years prior to the publication of this editorial, white Virginians had been utterly dependent on the labor—until very recently almost exclusively unpaid and forced—of African Americans for their prosperity.

Families Joined

The morning of December 27, 1877, dawned with the promise that a raw wintry day lay ahead in the Maryland–Virginia–Washington, D.C., region. Northeast winds were bringing clouds, rain, and freezing temperatures.[46]

It's likely the Gibson and Parker families didn't mind the conditions. For them, it was a time for joy, and not just because it was the holiday season. Matilda Gibson and Page Parker would wed that day in Washington. The two families, linked by geography and a business partnership, would now be forever joined through the bonds of marriage.

Page, twenty-one, and Matilda, eighteen, who would go on to have nine children, eventually took over the blacksmith business. Like his father before him, Page would eventually purchase several acres of land in Ilda. His first acquisition came in May 1881, when he bought a one-acre parcel from a man named Philip Howard. Five years later, a fire burned a storehouse on the property, along with the goods it contained and several outbuildings.

"The fire caught from the stove pipe, and there was no one home at the time, except Parker's wife and four little children," the *Fairfax Herald* reported. "There was no insurance on the property, and Parker estimates his loss at about $400."[47]

In April 1894, Parker purchased another parcel of a little more than an acre from James Caton. According to a deposition given by Parker's daughter Emma Robinson in 1931 during legal proceedings over dividing his property, this and the previous parcel combined contained not only the blacksmith shop but a "dwelling house, shrubbery and fruit trees, barn and several outbuildings."[48] In May 1904, Parker bought another two acres several hundred yards from the other parcels from Alice Kane.

Matilda went on to co-chair the Fairfax Colored Association, an influential group in the county. The association played a prominent role in advocating for schools for African American children, conducted voter registration efforts, coordinated membership drives for the National Association for the Advancement of Colored People, and organized various other fundraising efforts.[49]

When Page died in July 1905 at the age of forty-nine, Matilda and another blacksmith named H. L. Davis kept the blacksmith shop going. She later became the first African American resident of Ilda to have a telephone installed in her home.

It's only appropriate that Matilda was among the earliest residents of Ilda to gain a connection between the village and the wider world. According to family tradition, she had lent her name to the community. "Ilda," the story goes, was a contraction of "Matilda." That explanation, though not fully verified, is more plausible than any other that has come along. That's because no others have come along. There are no competing legends about the derivation of the name, no local landmarks by the name, and no other families in the area in which it or a variation of it appears.

It's easy to think of the name Ilda as nothing more than the answer to an obscure trivia question. But the fact that it became attached to the village and came to be used by Black and white residents alike is a strong indication of the influence the Gibson and Parker families had on the development of the community.

The Neighbors

The first reference to Ilda in a legal document so far uncovered came in 1897, on the marriage license of Wesley Gibson and Courtney Vass. The name first appears on an official map in 1915, on a U.S. Geological Service map of Fairfax.[50] By 1880, whether or not the name Ilda was in common use, the community was well-established. In addition to the Gibsons and Parkers, several other families lived in the area, according to census records.[51]

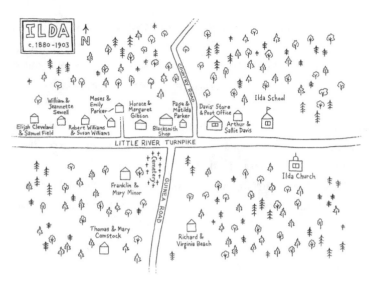

Map by Gregory Nemec

Robert Williams, who was now forty-five years old, remained in his home next to the Gibsons and Parkers. His sixty-five-year-old mother, Susan, was now living with him.

Elijah Cleveland, then twenty-three years old, lived west of the blacksmith shop on Little River Turnpike with his cousin Samuel Field. In the census, Cleveland listed his occupation as farmer, and Field worked as a shoemaker. Although Field was eight years older, Cleveland was listed as head of the household.

William H. Sewell, a fifty-five-year-old farmer, also lived in Ilda, with his wife, Jeanette, and their eleven-year-old daughter.

Down the street was Dr. Wilfred M. Mcleod, a physician, along with his wife, Alice, and their son. Mcleod's father was an Irish immigrant, and his mother was born in Maryland. They were living in Washington, D.C., when Wilfred was born.

South on Guinea Road a short distance away lived twenty-seven-year-old Thomas Comstock and his twenty-one-year-old wife, Mary, with their two-year-old son, Harry. Thomas was born in Connecticut and Mary in New York. They were a farm family, apparently among the northerners lured to Fairfax County by its agricultural potential.

Two generations of the Shaw family lived nearby and also were farmers. They had roots in Pennsylvania, New York, and New Jersey, so were presumably among the northerners who migrated to northern Virginia after the Civil War.

Nearby were Samuel L. Dove, thirty-seven, and his wife, Mary, twenty-eight. They had three children—two daughters and a son between the ages of four and nine. Samuel's occupation is listed as laborer on the census form.

Another member of the extended Dove family and area resident, Armstead Dove, had enlisted in the Seventeenth Virginia Infantry of the Confederate army on August 1, 1861, at Centreville, Virginia, with another Ilda landowner, Richard Beach. The two fought alongside each other in Company D for the duration of the war, and both were wounded at the Second Battle of Bull Run in August 1862. Beach was taken prisoner at Fairfax Court House at the war's end, just a few miles from his home.[52]

Listed as a laborer in the 1880 census, Beach lived across Little River Turnpike from the blacksmith shop, just to the south. In 1867 he married Armstead Dove's sister Virginia, and she took on the mellifluous name Virginia Beach—several years before the resort town of the same name on the Atlantic Ocean was incorporated.[53]

Across the street from the Beach family, on the southwest corner of the turnpike and Guinea Road, lived Mary and Franklin Minor. The couple were relatively new in town, having moved in just a few years earlier. Franklin was a lawyer. But it was in his personal, and decidedly not professional, experience with the law—as a defendant—that he made his mark on Ilda.

3

Transition

IN 1865, WILLIAM H. GOODING, the son of the William Gooding who had founded the family tavern and hotel business that preceded the development of Ilda, sold about eighty acres of land on the southwest side of the Little River Turnpike–Guinea Road intersection to Martin and Betty Gary. The couple were Irish immigrants who lived in Washington. But they apparently wanted no part of what was then very much rural living in Fairfax County. They never lived on the land they purchased but held onto it until 1874, when they sold it to Mary and Franklin Minor.

Actually, just to Mary. The deed to the property plainly states that it belongs to "Mrs. Mary Minor," and its conditions included the following: "that her husband Franklin Minor, shall have no right, title or interest vested [in] the land hereby conveyed."[1]

That's the first clue that something wasn't right with Franklin Minor.

It's unclear exactly when the Minors moved to Ilda. But if they weren't living on Mary's land before her ownership became official, then Franklin acted quickly after they settled in to become a menace to the community. By early fall 1874, he was already in legal trouble due to his interactions with his neighbors—in particular, Horace Gibson.

Minor, in fact, had threatened to kill Gibson.

On September 11, 1874, the *Fairfax News* reported that Gibson and Minor had appeared before a justice of the peace: "The former charged the latter with having made threats—by shooting or otherwise—against the life and person of the said Gibson." After several witnesses testified, the judge ordered Minor to keep the peace with his neighbors for a year, and fined him one hundred dollars.

Once again, Gibson had found success in the legal system. He had now already won at least two victories in the courts against white men.

Minor would, in time, move beyond simply threatening his neighbors to more serious offenses. Given his eventual record of lawbreaking, it's safe to assume he was a constant disruptive force in the neighborhood. And even when Minor wasn't harassing Ilda residents, both his hostility and the location of his home in the community must have been an irritant.

An intensive later investigation would determine that the eastern edge of the Minors' property contained the remains of enslaved African Americans for at least twenty-five years at the time Franklin and Mary arrived. Historical maps and plats produced in connection with legal proceedings indicate that the Minors' home was on the western section of the property, but their mere presence on that piece of land may have been a sore point for others—especially those, like the Gibsons and the Parkers, who may have lived among the enslaved on Guinea Road before purchasing their own plots of land.

Three Cemeteries

Finding a place to properly bury and memorialize their dead was a high priority among Black Americans, especially the enslaved. "Untimely death and dying marked the African American experience at its beginning—from mortality-plagued transatlantic voyages to the violence of forced labor and the privation of the slave quarters," wrote Tiffany Stanley in the *Atlantic* in 2016. "Surrounded by these unnecessary deaths, funeral ceremonies were an urgent and central rite in slave communities."[2]

Historical archaeologist Ross W. Jamieson has written that funerals also afforded the enslaved some degree of influence over their own cultural existence: "Funerals may have been one of the few times that antebellum slave communities could assume control of the symbolism around them, and thus create the dignity at death that negated the 'social death' of their slave status. In the burial practices of many cultures we see an area in which social groups are afforded the possibility of reviewing the past, and thus both reaffirming cultural consent for particular relationships, and also for disputing other power relationships."[3] Nevertheless, the enslaved faced restrictions on their funeral practices, just as they did in all aspects of life. "Even in death, blacks could not escape systematic racial proscription," writes Ira Berlin. "Whites no more wanted to be buried near black people than they wanted to mix with them in the same church or ride with them in the same coach."[4]

Throughout Virginia, severe restrictions were placed on gatherings of African Americans, even at funerals, for fear that they provided an opportunity to foment a rebellion of the enslaved. This was especially true after Nat Turner's Rebellion in 1831. White ministers were required to supervise African American funeral services.

Despite such regulations, which weren't always strictly enforced, funeral services became an integral part of the African

American experience, both for enslaved and free people. Part of the reason was that even white Virginians who accepted racist ideology as dogma and feared uprisings of the enslaved were leery of intruding on services for the deceased.

"In the majority of cases," writes Lynn Rainville in her study of African American cemeteries in central Virginia, "funerals were the only communal gathering permitted to enslaved individuals. . . . This rare opportunity, combined with African traditions that suggest that a proper funeral is required to send the deceased off to the afterlife, resulted in large gatherings that expressed both grief and celebration."[5] Such gatherings were usually held at night, often at midnight, because the enslaved had to work during the day. "It appears that on many plantations the enslaved community managed many if not all of their burial decisions," Rainville writes. That did not, however, prevent them from being accosted by slave patrols on occasion at their nighttime gatherings.[6]

White residents of Fairfax County had their own concerns about honoring their dead, especially after the Civil War. In 1866, the Ladies Memorial Association of Fairfax bought a plot of land in the heart of the city for the purposes of establishing a cemetery. It included this provision regarding who could be buried there: "In all cases such bodies shall be those of Confederate States' Soldiers, who fell in battle or died from wounds incident to and while they were in the service of the Confederate States, and who are now buried within the limits of said county, or who were citizens thereof at the time of death and are buried elsewhere."[7]

In October 1890, the Confederate Monument Association added a memorial to the unknown soldiers buried in the cemetery and troops from Fairfax who died on distant battlefields. The obelisk stands on top of a hill in the center of the Fairfax City Cemetery, which has since expanded to include members of the public with no connection to the Civil War.

The monument is stark and direct. "CONFEDERATE DEAD" reads the blunt inscription on its base. "From Fairfax to Appomattox, 1861–1865."

On an unseasonably warm early-December day in 2021, leaf blowers buzzed in the distance beyond the monument, as two groundskeepers went about their work. In the places where they had finished, it was difficult to find a leaf on the pristine, well-trimmed grass.

Across Main Street to the north sits a complex of offices and apartments called "The Mosby." Next to it is a small group of older businesses, including an auto repair shop and a bail bonds operation. (The county courthouse, as in days of old, is right up the street.) To the south, a parking garage for a postal building abuts the cemetery. Sirens occasionally wail in the distance, a reminder that a frenetic, sometimes tragic life goes on right outside the cemetery's gates.

But atop the hill, there is a powerful aura of peacefulness, the sense that one is not in suburbia but above it.

Most of the graves are simple, without extravagant ornamentation. Some are rough-hewn, others nearly fully eroded, and still others of more recent vintage incorporate such elements as photographs into the stones. "Together we made beautiful music," reads one. Well-known names in the county abound on the bigger markers—Fitzhugh, Dunn, Massey, Waple, Burke. Ilda resident Richard Beach is also buried here. Intermingled with the carved monuments are plain, flat stones memorializing the unknown and unnamed dead.

The Fairfax City Cemetery is beautiful and tranquil. It also is centered on a memorial to the Confederate cause. And taken as a whole, the cemetery itself is a monument to segregation and inequality.

African Americans were initially excluded from the cemetery both on the grounds of separation of the races and the extreme unlikelihood that they had actually fought and died for the Confederacy. So Black residents of the county sought a separate resting place for their dead. Horace Gibson and Moses Parker were particularly concerned with and involved in this effort. In 1868, they were among a small group of people who petitioned Fairfax County to allow the creation of a cemetery for African Americans.

As a result, Jermantown Cemetery was established, a mile outside of Fairfax City. The one-acre graveyard was less than half the size of the city cemetery.

A group called the Burial Sons and Daughters of Benevolence of Fairfax Court House, Virginia, oversaw the Jermantown Cemetery. Among its original trustees was Milton Brooks, the father of Margaret Brooks Gibson, wife of Horace Gibson.[8]

Sometime around 1870, the "Lodge No. 4 Sons & Daughters of Benevolence, Situated in Fairfax CO Va.," presented a petition to James Keith, a circuit court judge, asking him to appoint new trustees for the cemetery on the grounds that its oversight had "been very much neglected." They asked the judge to appoint Gibson, his son Strother, and James Henderson as new trustees. Strother, Henderson, and a man named James Roe did actually end up serving as trustees.[9] Years later, Fairfax County took over management of the cemetery.

The graveyard at Little River Turnpike and Guinea Road was altogether different from Jermantown Cemetery. It was characterized by its simplicity. Only one inscribed headstone has ever been found at the burial ground. The other graves, if marked at all, were indicated by simple fieldstones, the kind that years later would be mistaken for mere rocks or boundary markers.

This was not uncommon, for several reasons. Virginia law prohibited teaching African Americans to read or write. And even if an enslaved person was literate, it would have been challenging to find the time to carve an inscription in a fieldstone, which was very different from the marble or slate used on inscribed headstones.[10]

Transition

In 2006, columnist John Kelly of the *Washington Post* imagined the scene at the intersection this way:

> It's 1870 or 1880, and you are traveling in a horse-drawn carriage down Little River Turnpike toward Alexandria. The day is fine, and yours is the only cart on the road.
>
> And then: disaster. The iron rim of one wheel comes loose. You set the brake and hop from your seat. You are not superstitious, but you can't help but notice you have broken down next to a graveyard. It's a modest cemetery: no granite sarcophagi, no marble angels. But the fieldstones atop the mounded earth and the occasional carved headstone tell you that someone cares about it nonetheless.
>
> The insects sing in the trees as you start walking east in search of help. Soon you detect the scent of a bellows-driven fire and hear the clang of metal on metal. A blacksmith!
>
> Perhaps the graveyard was good luck.[11]

At least once, the scenario Kelly imagined played out in real life. On March 27, 1908, the *Fairfax Herald*'s Ilda correspondent reported that on "Friday evening, as Rev. F. A. Strother was hurrying home to plant some potatoes, the front axle of his buggy snapped and deposited him in the road. Fortunately, however, a blacksmith shop was near and he was able to have the damage repaired."[12]

Unfortunately, the graveyard's good luck did not extend to the people buried there. At least some of the African Americans interred in this small plot of land—less than an acre—had clearly endured unspeakable hardships. Even those who may not have been enslaved or, if they were, had not been abused by their enslavers lived lives of thankless hard labor, and they and their families faced the constant prospect of disease and death.

More than one hundred years later, remains uncovered at the site would show evidence of poor diet in the form of teeth that researchers concluded were in "extraordinarily bad shape." About one-third of the remains analyzed showed evidence of musculoskeletal stress. More than 40 percent of those buried at the Guinea Road Cemetery were infants and children.[13]

Available archaeological and historical evidence suggests the Guinea Road Cemetery was in use from as early as 1850 until 1868, when the Jermantown Cemetery was established. It is impossible to determine exactly who was buried there (and who may still be underneath Guinea Road, which has been widened several times), but the Goodings and Fitzhughs enslaved dozens of people for most of this period. If, indeed, the Gibsons and Parkers had moved into the area during the Civil War and lived in an African American shantytown, as oral tradition has it, it seems likely they would have witnessed burials of people they knew, if not their own family members. And the small cemetery at the crossroads of Ilda may have served as a lasting reminder of that experience.

Major Charges

Whether or not any of this was going through Horace Gibson's mind when he encountered Franklin Minor before and after the 1874 trial, Minor certainly continued to earn the enmity of Gibson and other Ilda residents. He may have succeeded in keeping the peace for the year he was ordered to do so in 1874, and maybe even for a few years after that. But by 1879 he was back in court, facing even more serious charges.

This time Minor didn't just threaten to shoot one of his neighbors. He actually did.

The court record of the case is filled with scrawled motions, summonses, and other filings, the handwriting faded and barely decipherable after years in storage. The documents are filled with cross-throughs and revisions, and characterized in many instances by what could charitably be described as archaic penmanship. Still, they make clear that the incident in question took place at the Little River Turnpike–Guinea Road intersection, and it involved Minor and Elijah Cleveland.

An affidavit with the names of Moses Parker, Brook Gibson, and Horace Gibson on it includes details of the incident:

> Frank Minor, on the 5th day of June, 1879 . . . in and upon one Elijah Cleveland, did make an assault [on] the said Elijah Cleveland, with a certain pistol, then and there loaded with gunpowder and leaden ball, feloniously and maliciously, did shoot the said Elijah Cleveland with the intent . . . then and there to maim, disfigure, disable and kill, against the peace and dignity of the Commonwealth of Virginia.

On June 12, a judge issued a warrant for Minor's arrest.

In the subsequent legal proceedings, Minor avoided conviction on the most serious charge he faced. A judge's message to the jury contained in court filings includes the following:

> The court instructs the jury that the jury which formerly tried the accused (Minor) upon this indictment by their silence respecting the charge of malicious shooting, entirely and altogether acquitted the accused of the offense of malicious shooting and it remains for the jury to consider the charge of unlawful shooting, or of assault and battery. They cannot under any possible contingency find the prisoner, Minor, guilty of malicious shooting, with intent, etc., as charged in the indictment.

Ultimately, a jury found Minor guilty of the unlawful shooting charge and sentenced him to six months in the county jail and a fine of one hundred dollars.

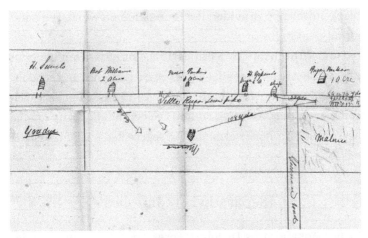

A hand-drawn plat from the 1879 trial of Franklin Minor shows the crime scene. (Courtesy of the Fairfax Circuit Court Historic Records Center)

At one point during the trial, Cleveland took the stand and discussed the interactions that led to the shooting. His weariness with Minor and the whole proceeding is evident in this exchange with Minor's attorney:

Q: Did you have a meeting with Minor between the time of cursing and abuse and the time of the shooting?
A: Yes, several days before the shooting.
Q: Why did you not demand an explanation of Minor at that time?
A: Because I did not feel like it.[14]

Elijah Cleveland was a white man. But Minor seemed to have a particular problem with African Americans. His future brushes with the law—and there would be more—involved confrontations with Black residents of Ilda, and later Washington, D.C.

While Minor made Ilda downright dangerous at times, there were multiple other ways it was rendered inhospitable for Black residents, despite the fact that Horace Gibson and Moses Parker's blacksmith shop provided the foundation on which the community was built.

Among the institutions critical to the success of any community in the late nineteenth century were churches and schools. Ilda would come to have both, but African Americans were welcome in neither. And that shifted the center of gravity for the descendants to more welcoming—if segregated—neighborhoods nearby.

Separation of Churches

In the 1960s and 1970s, Dr. John P. Forest spent fifteen years building a thriving dental practice in the Annandale area. Then the building in which he leased space went up for sale. He decided to try to combine an office and a home in one complex. He found the perfect piece of property on Little River Turnpike, just a little way east of Guinea Road. On August 1, 1977, he bought it.

It wasn't an ordinary plot of land, as evidenced by the deed, which transferred to Forest "all of that certain lot of ground and all the buildings thereon, known as the Ilda Church."[15]

Forest petitioned the Fairfax County Board of Zoning Appeals for permission to mingle home and dentistry at one location. That would involve demolishing the building that had been the church. "The property would have to be rehabilitated," his representative said at a zoning board hearing, "as the structure existing now is old. Originally, the structure was used as a church and was later converted to a residence. . . . [T]he existing structure would be removed."[16]

The board approved Forest's request, and the building was torn down. That marked the disappearance of the last of the pillars of Ilda.

At the time of the founding of the community, all of its residents, white and Black, had to travel to go to church. For a brief time, some of the white residents attended services at Wakefield Chapel on the western edge of Annandale, a short distance from Ilda. In the early 1900s, they began to push for a church of their own.

In June 1907, at a camp meeting in Ilda, came news that a resident, W. W. Smith, had agreed to donate an acre of land on which to erect a church. Now the only problem was raising the funds to build it. "No more worthy object could engage the attention and appeal to the liberality of a generous public than this," argued the *Fairfax Herald*. "This is a felt and imperative need at Ilda: a congregation of 150; a Sunday school of 60, and a church of 40 and no house, and the community unable to build such as is needed."[17]

The fundraising effort apparently paid off, because the cornerstone of the Methodist Episcopal Church South at Ilda was laid on September 26. Several ministers spoke at the celebration, the Fairfax Brass Band provided musical entertainment, and a "fine dinner" was served, raising seventy-five dollars.[18] The construction of the church was another sign that the community was developing, even if the inability of residents to fund it was an ominous sign. In 1893, Ilda residents had gained their own post office.[19] Now its white citizens would have their own house of worship.

They would have to be patient, though. "Work seems to be progressing slowly on the Methodist Church at Ilda, owing to various causes," the *Herald* reported on March 13, 1908.[20] The church wasn't completed until later that year. It clearly was a source of pride for white residents, and for concern and embarrassment if it failed to live up to its role as an indicator of the community's status. Within just a few years, it had apparently fallen into a state of disrepair.

"The Ilda Church, which has been an eyesore to the entire community and to passersby for so long a time," reported the *Herald* in 1914, "is now the most beautiful spot in all of Ilda after undergoing a coat of paint by Mr. George Daniels of Lincolnia."[21]

Ilda's Black residents likely never saw the inside of the Ilda Church. They weren't allowed to worship there. To them, it was just another building they had to pass on their miles-long trek to attend services at an African American church. At first, that meant going to either Fairfax or the Second Baptist Church of Falls Church, established in 1870. The latter excursion involved traveling seven miles from Ilda over country roads whose repair and maintenance was uneven at best and dependent on the commitment to upkeep of local residents who lived nearby.

The long trek may well have been worth the effort. Many Black Americans, who had been prevented from practicing their religion while enslaved, preferred to establish their own churches, with African American ministers, rather than follow the spiritual leadership of white preachers.

Churches "provided a place of refuge and financial support for many blacks; a haven to express opinions and to practice leadership that had been denied by enslavement," wrote Marion Dobbins, a public historian in Fairfax County who grew up in Merrifield, in 2014. "Churches allowed blacks to talk openly about politics without fear of retribution, voting issues, civil injustice, harassment, and other concerns within the community. [They] also served as a place to teach their children how to become young adults and citizens."[22]

To create such spaces, African Americans had to start from scratch. The Second Baptist Church of Falls Church had its beginning in a two-room log cabin. In 1872, members of the congregation raised money and built a church with hand-hewn timber and locally forged nails. Women helped finance the effort by picking blackberries and walking to and from Washington, D.C.'s Georgetown neighborhood to sell them at a farmer's market.[23]

In the early 1890s, prospects among Black residents of Ilda and other far-flung parts of Fairfax County for a somewhat less arduous trip to worship services brightened, when some of the sons and daughters of the founders of the Second Baptist Church banded together to establish an African American church in Merrifield. They had already been holding services in tents and homes nearby with the help of itinerant preachers. In 1891, a group of men paid five dollars for a small plot of land for the purposes of establishing the First Baptist Church of Merrifield. A board of trustees was created, and members of the faith community built a wooden platform to hold services outside when weather permitted.[24]

In 1895, a new church was dedicated, complete with a bell that church members raised $195 to purchase. That building was replaced in 1962, and the bell was lost. But it turned up in the early 2000s and sits on the grounds of the church, which is still in operation.[25]

The First Baptist Church is a red brick building, painted gleaming white on its sides, its steeple rising high into the sky. The landscaping is simple and unadorned but well-tended. Today, the church sits across the street from Lube-It (promising ten-minute oil changes) and a scrap metal shop. A hodgepodge of other businesses surround it: a gas station, a Silver Diner restaurant, a barber shop, and Namaste Market, an Indian grocery store.

Across Gallows Road, now a major thoroughfare, loom the high-rise apartment buildings, parking garages, restaurants, and shops of the Mosaic District. First Baptist is barely visible from the road, but up close, it stands almost in defiance of the commercialization around it. The church seems not only out of place, but out of time. It's almost impossible to imagine what this area was like when it was a muddy enclave of wood-framed houses known as Slabtown.

"You know when you saw lumber, and the slabs come off the side?" remembered Everett Robey, who grew up between Merrifield and Ilda in the early twentieth century, in an oral history interview in the early 1980s. "Well, the roads was so bad out there that they, in the wintertime, they couldn't hardly get on their horses and wagons. They made a slab road, and so they called [it] Slabtown. And then later on, when they got this post office, they changed it to Merrifield. And boy, they'd get mad if you called it Slabtown."[26]

Today, by mentally blocking out everything around First Baptist, it's possible to see it as what it must have been at the time it was built: a majestic monument to faith and perseverance. "Moving From Great to Greater" reads a sign in front of the building.

"I believe we are still a very powerful force in the Greater Merrifield community," said Rev. Dr. Paul Shepard, First Baptist's pastor, in 2022. "The members are committed to the mission and mandate of Jesus Christ." Many of those members no longer live in Merrifield. But "these are people who love the church. They love the history of the church."[27]

In late 2021, visitors to the First Baptist website were greeted with a carousel of images and messages, including one titled "PRESS ON." Beneath it was this Bible verse from St. Paul's letter to the Philippians: "Forgetting what is behind and straining toward what is ahead, I press on toward the goal to win the prize for which God has called me heavenward in Christ Jesus."

"Press On" could serve as an apt motto for the African Americans of Merrifield and surrounding areas of Fairfax County, like Ilda. And not just in finding a place to practice their faith, but to educate their children. The deed to the First Baptist Church, for example, contained a significant stipulation: the land was to be used solely as a house of worship, and not for any other purpose—such as a school. So as challenging as it was for Black residents to establish churches, schools would be an even tougher task—and one where segregation and inequality would disadvantage African American children and deny them opportunities afforded to white students for the better part of a century.

Segregated Schools

In 1896, the U.S. Supreme Court handed down its landmark decision in *Plessy v. Ferguson,* upholding the constitutionality of "separate but equal" public facilities for whites and Blacks. The "separate" part was already deeply entrenched in Virginia and throughout the South. "Equal" was another matter. The core doctrine of separation of the races would play out prominently in education until the Supreme Court's 1954 decision in *Brown v. Board of Education* that separate schools for Black and white children were inherently unequal. (And in Virginia, state officials fought a campaign of "massive resistance" to the latter decision for years.)

In the late nineteenth century, white residents were very concerned about establishing and supporting schools. But most were at best indifferent about the education of Black children. By 1882, the county had five schools offering multiple grades of education for white students. In 1874, two white Merrifield residents had donated land "to erect a building to be used as a school home," provided "that if school be kept and maintained for any other than white children of the neighborhood, then said shall revert to the grantor with the same right as if the deed has not been given."[28]

Officials also approved the creation of what were called "colored schools." But African American families were largely left to their own devices in setting up and operating them and had to make do with whatever they could come up with in the way of facilities.

The Merrifield school for Black children wasn't established until 1882. Classes were not held in a formal school building but possibly in someone's home. In 1897, the local school board purchased land to build a one-room schoolhouse. It was located near the First Baptist Church, on what is now a parking lot for a

The Merrifield Colored School, established in 1882, in a 1942 photo. (Courtesy of the Fairfax County Public Schools)

Homewood Suites hotel. A second schoolhouse with two rooms was built in 1939 due to overcrowding in the older school.[29]

Conditions at each facility were primitive.

"There was a pot-bellied stove in there and we had to walk and sometimes it would be so cold that when we got there the teacher would have a basin of water for us to put our hands in, you know, so that we wouldn't freeze up until we could get the circulation back in our hands," recalled one former student. "We had secondhand books from the white schools and half the pages weren't there and it just wasn't really good. I don't ever remember ever having a new book."[30]

"The schools for Blacks were in the most dilapidated conditions," a local historian has written. "All were frame buildings and old, with outbuildings to serve toilet needs. Most Black schools had no source of drinking water on the grounds; it had to be brought in from a neighbor's well."[31]

In 1905, John F. Lewis, the Republican candidate for governor of Virginia, backed a plan to provide free textbooks to students across the state. The *Fairfax Herald* engaged in a befuddling math exercise in voicing its opposition to the idea. "The negroes of this county," the paper's editors opined, "constitute 26 percent of the school enrollment, [and] they own 4 percent of the property in the county. This means that out of every $26 worth of books furnished to negroes, the white people would pay $22 of it; and the negroes would pay $4." The paper found "the ambition to make classical scholars" of African Americans threatening, wondering who would be left to do the "hewing of wood, the drawing of water and the hoeing of corn."

The *Herald* wrapped it all up by building a formidable straw man bedecked in the growing Lost Cause mythology of the Civil War: "The Confederate soldier is not mentioned in the Republican platform. The Democratic Party gives to the old soldiers $300,000 per year. Do the Republicans propose to take this money to provide free books for the negroes?"[32]

Racial inequities and indignities abounded when it came to education. In 1913, Black teachers in the Falls Church School District, which included Merrifield and Ilda, were granted a pay raise from thirty to thirty-five dollars per month. Two years earlier, salaries for three newly hired white teachers in the district had been set at fifty dollars per month. Pay for white teachers hadn't been as low as thirty dollars since the late 1800s.

During a 1913 school board meeting, M. D. Hall, superintendent of the Falls Church School District, presented a bill for the expenses of L. H. Jackson, who had served as a delegate to a Black teachers' convention in Norfolk, Virginia. The board voted to refuse reimbursement.[33]

When school was in session—and the school year for Black students was one month shorter than the one for white students—Merrifield was a daily destination for Ilda's Black children. It was an arduous trek that involved crossing a log footbridge across Accotink Creek, which frequently flooded, and climbing a large hill on Woodburn Road on the way back home in the afternoon. This was more than a nuisance. It was an ongoing lesson for young African Americans in Ilda that they were second-class citizens in a community their parents and grandparents had helped establish, and that was getting farther and farther from its roots.

Meanwhile, the Ilda community clamored for a school of its own—the white community, that is. On September 29, 1892, residents convinced the local school board to hold a meeting at Ilda to consider the prospect. "Demand urgent," reads the minutes of the meeting.

The minutes also record the meeting's location: "Gibson's shop." The board and the community literally launched the effort to build a whites-only school at a business owned and operated by the African American families who founded Ilda.[34]

The school was built in 1897. It stood on Little River Turnpike, just a short distance east of the Guinea Road intersection, across the turnpike from the Ilda Church. Meeting minutes from a school board discussion held at Ilda in December 1897 show the board approved payment of one hundred dollars to a contractor for completing work on the school, and arranged for a local resident to provide firewood for the building at a rate of two dollars per month.[35]

The Ilda School had two rooms, one for grades one through four, and the other for fifth through eighth grades. African American students had to walk by both the church and the school on their way to their school in Merrifield. "That was really a shame," said Everett Robey. "They were good . . . people, and right around the corner we had a school. Those children walked all the way to Merrifield, backwards and forwards. Better than three miles [each way]. And the school was right there at Ilda."[36]

Along the way, those students regularly had to put up with acts of ignorance and racism, big and small.

The Ilda School "used to have minstrel shows," Robey remembered. "Used to black up, you know? I wasn't in any of them, but they did have them there. My sister blacked up one time and said a colored girl met her in the road and said, 'Too bad y'alls ain't Black.'"

Residents of Ilda and surrounding areas continued to petition for an African American school closer to where they lived for years. In 1922, for example, nine families with thirty-seven children aged fourteen and younger signed a petition to the Fairfax County School Board to establish a school near Ravensworth, which would have been more convenient for Ilda children. It was denied. In 1949, the board was advised that six acres of land near Ilda was available to be used as the site of a Black school. According to the minutes of a board meeting, "there was discussion of the need of a colored school site in this area, the opinion being expressed that a development progressing in this area might justify a school. The Chairman appointed . . . a committee to investigate the proposed school site in this area." The school was never built.[37]

The extreme inequity of segregated schools was surely a factor in the long-term decline of Ilda. Without a place to worship or attend school, the community became at best an extremely inconvenient place for Black residents to live. The message was clear: You belong in segregated communities elsewhere in the county, such as Merrifield.

In 1913, the Ilda School burned down. It was not rebuilt. The school board arranged to pay fifteen dollars for three months' rent at the Ilda Church to finish the school year.

Ilda would not have its own school again for more than forty years. In 1951, the school board discussed the possibility of finding a site in Ilda for a "negro high school," but the idea never came to fruition. In October 1952, the board adopted a resolution to secure a site for an elementary school there, "due to the continuing overcrowding of the Fairfax Elementary School, largely as a result of the increasing number of pupils coming from the Ilda area."[38] That school arrived in 1955.

The school was called Wakefield Forest Elementary, after the housing development in which it was located. As with all white Fairfax County public schools, Black children were not allowed to attend. That didn't change at Wakefield Forest until 1965, after Virginia finally gave up its fight against complying with the *Brown v. Board of Education* decision. Curiously, though, when Black students finally walked through the doors of Wakefield Forest, they were met with another form of segregation: boys and girls were taught in separate classrooms. According to an official school history, "Principal Glenn Wells felt that boys and girls learned differently and that boys would progress faster if they did not have to compete with girls academically." That experiment lasted until 1973 and was not repeated at other county schools.[39]

Today, Wakefield Forest Elementary School sits a short distance from Little River Turnpike, across the road from where the Ilda School was located. "We believe in creating a safe, inclusive, and challenging environment where diversity is valued," reads the "Our Beliefs" section of the school's website.[40]

End of the Century

At the turn of the twentieth century, Ilda was a thriving community. With the establishment of a post office, church, and school, it had arrived. And, as had been the case since Horace Gibson and Moses Parker opened their blacksmith shop, its location put it at the center of county activities—at least for its white residents. The community had its own general store, operated by Arthur Davis, just down the road from the blacksmith shop. The shop would remain in operation for a few more years, as the cobblestones of Little River Turnpike continued to wreak havoc on wagons and buggies. But road improvements were becoming a big priority for Fairfax County residents. Many were so turned off by the county's turnpikes that they favored what came to be called "shun-pikes"—narrow, muddy roadways that ran parallel to the turnpikes.[41]

"We have received an invitation to be present at the good roads, agriculture and temperance rally to be held at Ilda, Fairfax County, May 26th, under the auspices of the Fairfax Good Roads Association and the Anti-Saloon League of Northern Virginia," wrote the "Local Brevities" columnist in the *Alexandria Gazette* in 1910. (Just below, the same column touted Duffey's Pure Malt Whiskey, for "medicinal purposes," of course.)[42]

The *Gazette* was filled with such references to Ilda, from the serious (such as news of rallies of one sort or another and revival meetings led by itinerant preachers) to the mundane ("It has been whispered around town that one of our young Ilda farmers will lead to the altar one of Alexandria's beauties").[43] Other newspapers focused on Ilda, too. The *Fairfax Herald* referenced the community more than six hundred times in its pages between 1886 and 1964. In 1912, a legal advertisement for a real estate auction described Ilda as "a community which is being rapidly built up."[44]

But for the Gibson and Parker families, opportunities beckoned elsewhere. Horace and Margaret Gibson's son Strother and his wife, Martha, lived for a time on the land that Strother's parents had purchased on Little River Turnpike. Then, in 1884, he bought his own piece of property on nearby Braddock Road and built a log cabin on it. He and Martha later put down roots in the Fairfax area. He became a trustee not only of the Jermantown Cemetery but of Mount Calvary Baptist Church in the city.

Another son, Wesley Gibson, worked as a stonemason in Falls Church. In 1886, he and his wife purchased land in Merrifield and made their home there before moving to Washington, D.C. Wesley's brother, John Edward, moved to Philadelphia and started several successful businesses. Two other sons of Horace and

Margaret, Brook and George, bought 104 acres of land near Ilda and began farming it. After Brook died at the age of thirty-five in 1897, George sold his property and moved to Ansonia, Connecticut. He took a job in nearby Bridgeport. Other relatives would ultimately join him in Ansonia.

Likewise, Moses Parker Jr. moved to Rhode Island and lived there until he died in 1891. So did his brother James, after farming for a time in Ilda on land he inherited from Robert Williams. He worked as a cook and eventually ran his own catering business.[45]

Ilda's character, along with that of the rest of the county, was changing. And the more obstacles that Black county residents overcame, the more were thrown in their way. Post-Reconstruction racism became more overt, and more virulent.

In Falls Church, Black residents were segregated in three communities: the Hill, Southgate Subdivision, and Gravel Banks. By 1873, African Americans made up 232 of the total of 632 residents of Falls Church. White residents, threatened by the possibility of sharing power with their African American neighbors, voted to change the town's borders to cut off the Black sections. "Probably only the viciously racist attacks by the county newspapers and the physical violence they may have inspired was more detrimental than the denial of political rights to Falls Church Blacks by the racially motivated boundary change," historian Patrick Reed has written.[46]

Worse was to come. After Reconstruction, the Democratic Party gained control of Virginia politics and maintained its grip for decades. The conservative Democrats feared the growing political strength of Black voters and relied on corrupt practices to maintain control of government operations even in areas where they were in the minority. They began openly campaigning for a state constitutional convention with the central purpose of institutionalizing fraudulent practices that deprived African Americans of voting rights. "In other words, the concern of many

Virginia conservatives was not to eliminate the corruption, but to legalize it," according to Reed.[47]

In 1888, Democrats pushed a referendum on holding a state-wide constitutional convention. It failed, with fewer than 6 percent of Fairfax County voters backing the idea. By 1897, the county's approval figure had risen to 32 percent, and in 1900 it stood at 43 percent. But statewide, 56 percent of voters favored the measure, so the convention took place in 1901–2. Delegates approved provisions requiring that every voter give, in their own handwriting, their name, age, and address, and "answer on oath any and all questions affecting his qualifications as an elector, submitted to him by the officers of registration." Prospective voters also would be required to pay a poll tax of $1.50.[48]

These measures were clearly aimed at limiting participation in elections, particularly by Black voters, and they had their intended effect. In Fairfax County, fewer than one-third of the people who had voted in 1900 did so in 1904. In post–Civil War elections, between 15 and 25 percent of the county's population had voted. After 1902, the figure dropped to between 6 and 10 percent. That enabled Democrats to keep a stranglehold on local politics.

Over the next several decades, Fairfax County would change dramatically, and not just politically. Fewer than thirteen thousand people lived in the county in 1870. By 1900, the total had reached 18,580, an increase of more than 40 percent. County officials were convinced, and sought to convince others, that its future was bright, especially as the federal government and its workforce grew. In 1907, the board of supervisors published a book touting the agricultural, industrial, financial, cultural, and religious attributes of the county.[49]

"Verily, Fairfax County, old in its history, and hoary in its traditions, is throbbing with a new life of activity and enterprise," the report declared. "Within the last few years," it went on, "the county has made marvelous industrial progress. Miles of electric railway have been built, and many more miles are still being constructed and projected. The great trunk line railways, running through the county, have recently double-tracked their ways, thereby doubling their capacity for handling the through and local traffic. Three banks have been recently organized, and are all now doing a large and flourishing business."

Still, farming was the central economic activity, and dairy farming led the way. "The great bulk of the milk supply of the cities of Washington and Alexandria comes from Fairfax," the book reported. "Every morning thousands of gallons of Fairfax milk, by train, trolley and wagon, enter these cities."

The book noted that there were sixty-one churches in the county, "representing all shades of religious belief." Just not all shades of worshipers. The figure cited referred only to white churches.

Double-Barreled Danger

Ilda, like the rest of Fairfax County, was changing as the nineteenth century drew to a close. But some things, unfortunately, stayed the same.

"A DASTARDLY CRIME," read the headline on the front page of the *Richmond Planet* on October 8, 1898. Below it was this brief story in the African American newspaper, datelined "Fairfax Court House, October 4": "Franklin Minor shot Horace Gibson (colored) early this morning near here. They had some dispute over damages claimed by Gibson to have been done by Minor's horse. Gibson received both loads from a double-barreled shotgun, one in the shoulder, the other in the abdomen. His condition is regarded as serious. Minor is now in jail. His preliminary trial has been postponed for ten days to await the result of the wounds inflicted."[50] In other words, they were waiting to see if Gibson would die. He did not.

For at least the second time, Minor had threatened violence against Gibson, and this time he had followed through. Minor was formally charged on October 17, and released on nine hundred dollars bail.[51] The court records from the case are lost, but apparently he was once again tried twice for offenses related to the incident. In March 1899, the *Alexandria Gazette* reported that Minor's second trial would take place during the Fairfax County Court's March term.[52]

There are no further records of or reports on the outcome of Minor's trial. But he didn't stop getting into trouble involving weapons and threats. On October 24, 1899, he was arrested in Washington on charges of carrying a concealed weapon. Minor, in the course of dropping off his horse at a stable, pulled a gun on the African American employees there. "HIS HIP POCKET WAS LOADED," reads the headline on the *Washington Post* report on the arrest. Minor "exhibited the weapon to the dismay of the negroes, one of whom reported the matter to the police."[53]

Two months later, a judge in Washington, at the urging of Minor's daughter, Virginia, signed an order committing him to an insane asylum. Minor, his daughter said, was suffering from "senile dementia."[54]

Gibson not only survived the shooting at Minor's hands but lived another fourteen years, dying in 1912 at the age of ninety-five. Moses Parker died in 1887 at sixty-two. The blacksmith shop closed in 1910.

By the late 1800s, Gibson and Parker between them owned more than four hundred acres of property, and several of their children were landholders as well. It was, a family historian wrote, "quite remarkable for Blacks to accumulate such wealth given all the hardships they had to suffer and overcome."[55]

Minor died in 1901 in Washington. Over the next 120 years, the property he and his wife lived on, and the cemetery it contained, would pass through the hands of several real estate developers and homeowners. After a series of twists and turns in that process, it would become the centerpiece of an epic battle involving road construction, the pace of development in Fairfax County, the effects of systemic racism, the legacy of the Gibsons and Parkers, and the history of Ilda.

4

Segregation

ON A MARCH SUNDAY in 1923, Rev. J. C. Trasher of the Methodist Episcopal Church South in Fairfax was giving his farewell sermon. The congregation was no doubt rapt with attention because Trasher was a beloved spiritual leader.

Suddenly, the back doors of the church flew open. In marched ten robed and hooded members of the Ku Klux Klan. They strode up to the pulpit and theatrically presented the pastor with a purse containing fifty dollars in gold. It was, at the very least, a conspicuous show of strength to the community.[1]

The Klan had been reborn in 1915 and would make its presence felt in Fairfax County for the next several decades. By the 1920s, Klan members were openly flaunting their white supremacist ideology, burning crosses at public events and participating in funerals at Fairfax City Cemetery. They were also freely taking part in such activities as marching in local parades and participating in county fairs.[2]

Their covert activities were more threatening. Edwin B. Henderson, an influential African American leader who was instrumental in launching the first rural chapter of the NAACP in Falls Church, received more than one hundred threatening letters at the time, including one in 1915 that read, in part: "Some night when you are peacefully dreaming . . . of the charming BABOONS that you have been instructing, and sniffing in the delightful odor exuding from their bodies, you will be rudely awakened by GHOSTS . . . and after you have been gagged, you will be born to a tree nearby, tied, stripped and given thirty lashes on your ETHIOPIAN back, and left to be found by some passer-by."[3]

While only a relatively small number of white Fairfax County residents went to such extremes, nostalgia for the old Confederacy ran high. Col. John Mosby became a folk hero whose exploits were celebrated among county residents, in local ceremonies and in school texts. His name was attached to buildings, monuments, and housing developments. Having the name "Lee" conferred great political advantage on candidates for office. Gen. William Henry Fitzhugh Lee, who took up residence at Ravensworth after the Civil War, won a seat in the Virginia Senate and was later elected to Congress for three terms. Even many of the northerners who settled in the county after the war became converts to the Lost Cause, embracing such traditions as the rebel yell and singing "Dixie."[4]

In 1915, after Virginia enacted a law permitting housing segregation, the Falls Church town council took up a proposed ordinance that would have created designated areas of the city for white and Black residents. African Americans would have had to move to the small section assigned to them, even if they already made their homes in the proposed whites-only section. The Falls Church chapter of the NAACP hired lawyers to challenge the constitutionality of the law, and the council backed down.[5]

The embrace of the Lost Cause mythology played out not only in political and cultural life but in religious life as well. The Ilda Church, like the one in Fairfax that Klan members invited themselves into, was part of the Methodist Episcopal Church South denomination. That made it very different from the nearby Wakefield Chapel, which was also Methodist—without the "South."

The Wakefield Chapel area and Ilda were just a short distance apart. Some Ilda residents attended services at Wakefield Chapel before their church was built. And white children from Wakefield went to the Ilda School for several years. But while the two churches were physically close, they had limited interaction in the early twentieth century. Partly, that was due to local geography. While the churches weren't far apart as the crow flies, getting from one to the other involved an arduous trip through dense forests. But that kind of obstacle didn't stop people from traveling similar distances for other reasons—such as the trek Ilda's Black children had to make to go to school in Merrifield.

The more significant factor was the allegiance to the South spelled out in the Ilda Church's denomination. "The fact that the Ilda congregation was Methodist Episcopal South indicates that theirs was a fierce, defensive pride of the defeated Confederacy, an attitude that loomed large in northern Virginia for generations after the war. This was in contrast to the many landowners in Wakefield who were ex-Union soldiers or anti-slavery advocates," reads a history of Wakefield Chapel published by Fairfax County in 1977.[6]

Rev. Frank A. Strother, the first pastor of the Ilda Church, had been a chaplain under Mosby's command during the Civil War. He was among a group of Mosby's men captured by Gen. George Custer at Front Royal, Virginia. They were to be hanged but escaped on the night before their scheduled execution.[7]

Conversely, Rev. Elhanan Wakefield, the Methodist preacher who helped found Wakefield Chapel, and for whom it was named, fought on the Union side. He was wounded at the First Battle of

Bull Run. In a 1976 interview, Lowell T. Wakefield, his grandson, who lived in Fairfax County, expressed dismay at learning of his grandfather's allegiance. "I was a little disappointed," he said. "Apparently the old gentleman served, obviously, on the Yankee side, and my sentiments really don't lie there."[8]

Old School

When Martha Gibson died in 1926, she had made enough of an impact on the county to merit an obituary in the *Fairfax Herald*. But in a nod to the growing backlash against equal rights for all races, the remembrance read, "She was one of the old school of negroes and her death is sincerely regretted."[9] Likewise, when Strother Gibson died just a few months later, he also was given the "old school of negroes" accolade, and characterized as a man "who respected himself and had the respect and confidence of his white neighbors." The newspaper also referred to the couple as "Aunt Martha" and "Uncle Strother."[10]

The new school of African Americans were to be taught their place through the imposition of Jim Crow laws. These upended what had been at least relative comity between the races in the area. William West, who was born in 1874 and became a longtime teacher in Black schools in Fairfax County, remembered in an interview conducted when he was one hundred years old how the situation changed at the turn of the century.[11]

Having performed well in elementary school as a child, West traveled to Washington, D.C., by train every day to attend high school, since there was no African American high school in Fairfax County (and there wouldn't be one for decades). In the late 1880s, there were no restrictions on travel based on race. "I could go in the car and sit anywhere I wanted, anywhere I'd find a seat," he said. Indeed, white commuters on the train befriended him and chatted with him on their daily rides.

Then in 1899, the rules changed, and the railway required African American passengers to sit in a separate car. "It was just a law, and we just had to take it," West said. "I was subject to it for 50 years."

As time went on, Fairfax County's proximity to Washington made for unusually demeaning segregation practices. In the District of Columbia, for example, African Americans could sit in whatever seats they liked on public transportation. But once buses reached the middle of bridges crossing over into Northern Virginia, Black riders had to get up and move to the rear.

"I would not sit in the Jim Crow seats while in the District," E. B. Henderson later recalled. "On one occasion when I refused to move when we entered Virginia at the Key Bridge, I was forcibly put off the bus." That situation wouldn't legally change until the practice was ruled unconstitutional in 1946.

Throughout the first half of the twentieth century, affinity for the old Confederacy and defensiveness about being on the losing side in the Civil War steadily grew. Those who fought for the preservation and extension of slavery were depicted as actually being on the right side of history. In 1928, Mary Millan composed a poem in honor of Confederate Memorial Day in Fairfax County. The first two stanzas read:

> Each year when Nature robes in green
> This mound of sacred dust,
> We come to scatter flowers here
> For those whose cause was just.
> These heroes gave their precious lives
> For a cause that's now called "lost,"
> They gave their all for Southland
> And counted not the cost.[12]

The cause was always lost. Now, in popular memory, it was just.

This shift occurred even as some local residents could remember the reality of the war, because they had lived through it. In February 1942, the *Fairfax Herald* reported that Mary Katherine Johnson, "probably the oldest colored resident of the county, died last week at her home at Ilda." Johnson, who was 101, was born into slavery in 1841 on a plantation in Goochland County, Virginia. She and her husband moved to Ilda shortly after its founding, and she had lived there ever since.[13]

Around midcentury, the affinity for the Confederacy accelerated further in and around Fairfax. In November 1951, the *Washington Post* reported on the curious rise in the display of Confederate paraphernalia, which hadn't been seen in almost one hundred years. "The Confederate flag has been especially conspicuous in nearby Virginia," the paper reported. "One was hanging in the auditorium of the Fairfax Village Library at a recent assembly dance." About three hundred students at Fairfax High School, attended by Ilda's white residents, were seen sporting Confederate forage caps. The school band was selling them for three dollars apiece as a fundraiser.[14]

Bust and Boom

While Fairfax County was regressing in terms of race relations, progress of another sort couldn't be stopped. Although the Great Depression hit Fairfax County hard, like the rest of the country, it also touched off a population boom that would grow stronger as the century unfolded.

President Franklin Roosevelt's creation of an alphabet soup of federal agencies to address the nation's economic crisis and create jobs for those out of work resulted in an influx of federal employees to the Washington area. They sought to live where land and homes were cheap, and Fairfax County fit the bill. Between 1930 and 1950, the county's population would quadruple. (It had taken 140 years, starting in 1790, for its population to double.) The new inhabitants, by and large, came from elsewhere in the country, causing Fairfax County to become less rural, less like the rest of Virginia, and more like its own city.[15]

That put communities like Ilda in an awkward position. Their proximity to Washington would change their character fundamentally. The growth, as always, put pressure on the county's transportation systems—especially its roads, as the automobile emerged as the primary suburban mode of travel.

In 1924, the Ford Motor Company, in conjunction with the U.S. Agriculture Department's Bureau of Public Roads, produced a short silent film called *The Road to Happiness*. It featured a fictitious, rural "Clay County" with rutted, muddy, nightmarishly poor roads. Fairfax County apparently provided an example of such conditions, because the movie was filmed there. President Calvin Coolidge made a cameo appearance, presenting Bob, a farm boy, with a college scholarship for an essay reading, in part, "Good roads and the family car give the farmer's family social advantages and make possible a consolidated school and central church for the farm district. The farmer can move his crops in accordance with the market, rather than the condition of the roads."

Bob becomes a highway engineer and returns home to make his vision of a modernized county a reality. New roads are built, and suddenly motor cars appear. "Won't the school kids be tickled when these old roads are improved?" he says, as images of children, horse-drawn wagons, and motorized vehicles sharing a paved road at the same time flash by.[16]

Fairfax County had taken over management and maintenance of Little River Turnpike in 1896, and tolls on the road became a thing of the past. In the 1920s, Virginia governor Harry Byrd directed significant state funds to pave over dirt roads with asphalt and build its first highways.

In May 1922, the county undertook a major reconstruction and paving of Little River Turnpike from Alexandria through Ilda to Fairfax Court House, at a cost of $200,000. There was a last-minute contract snafu over whether the road would be widened to sixteen or eighteen feet, the first of many such battles. The new turnpike "will be an important link in the chain of roads now being constructed and will shorten the distance between Alexandria and Fairfax by several miles," the *Washington Post* reported. "The present road is virtually impassable."[17]

By 1928, twenty-five of the thirty-four communities shown on maps of Fairfax County were connected to Washington by hard-surfaced roads.[18]

In 1932, county officials announced that the Virginia Department of Highways had allocated $146,000 to convert fifty miles of dirt roads in Fairfax County to hard surfaces. That included upgrading Woodburn Road from its intersection with Gallows Road in Merrifield to where it met with Little River Turnpike in Ilda. It would not be the last paved road connecting the two communities.[19]

In 1923, Hatcher and Lillian Ankers moved to a farm in Merrifield on an unnamed dirt road that was so rutted it was extremely difficult to traverse in bad weather. It was hardscrabble living, but whenever anyone would ask Hatcher where he lived, he would respond, "Why, on Prosperity Avenue, of course."[20] While that story may be apocryphal, Prosperity Avenue did come to be the name of a road that eventually extended from Merrifield to Ilda, near the spot where the school and a general store had been located. The winding, hilly road ends at Little River Turnpike, a short distance from Woodburn Road and just a few hundred yards from the Guinea Road intersection.

By the early 1920s, J. G. Dunn, who already operated a store in Ilda, had opened up a garage. He sold both in 1925, when he moved to Alexandria. In 1933, James Norfolk combined the general store and gas station he then owned into one operation providing everything from men's and women's clothing to automobile tires. "In this phase of the business Mr. Norfolk has won a large clientele of discriminating women and has concentrated his activity for the benefit of the group of residents here who appreciate the best in service and satisfaction," the *Fairfax Herald* reported.[21]

Meanwhile, other modern amenities were on their way to the village. "The Ilda community is working to secure electric lights," the *Herndon Observer* reported. "It is stated that the greater number of the necessary subscribers have been secured and that only a few more are needed to bring this valuable service to Ilda."[22]

As Fairfax County continued to grow, it created a school board and a health department. In 1935, the latter unit reported that about twenty-five thousand white people and just fewer than five thousand African Americans lived in the county. More than 80 percent of the population lived outside of incorporated towns, and those who did live in them were often dependent on farmers for their livelihood. Dairy farming still dominated, but commercial hog and chicken operations were on the rise. Fully 65 percent of the county's land was in farms, surrounded by "beautiful forests of hardwood trees."[23]

Other businesses were springing up in Ilda based on the county's development. In 1930, local landowner John W. Rust leased ten acres of his property for use as a stone quarry. An expert had pronounced it to be "of the best quality for building purposes."[24] But the stone was used for more than buildings. In 1937, a hunk of granite from the site was hauled to the Truro Church in Fairfax City to hold a bronze plaque commemorating the exploits of John Mosby.[25]

The news that came out of Ilda in this period was mostly agriculture-related. In 1930, the focus was on a mysterious "bean rain" that had fallen on Ilda's farmlands. Fairfax County agricultural agent H. B. Doerr was on the case immediately. He gathered up some of the "beans," and brought them to the Agriculture Department in Washington for analysis. It turned out they were seeds of sour gum trees that starlings and blackbirds had consumed. They feasted on the pulpy covering of the seeds, then spit out mouthfuls of the seeds themselves. Hence the mysterious "rain."[26]

Eight years later, Doerr, now out of his official position, had land use concerns of a different nature. He went before the county board of supervisors to inform them that "the people of his community had been advised that a colored man had recently attempted to purchase some land in the vicinity between Fairfax and Ilda . . . for the purpose of establishing a colored cemetery." Doerr presented a petition he and twenty-four of his neighbors had signed, demanding that the board take "immediate action" to put a stop to such an effort. Board members advised Doerr that they had no authority to prevent the establishment of cemeteries.[27]

People continued to stay in the county because of its rural character, and more moved in because they were attracted to it. Washington lawyer Edward Howrey and his wife, Jane, for example, purchased the Oak Hill house and property near Ilda in 1935 because, he later wrote in his autobiography, they "longed to live in the country where we could have horses and dogs." The estate was then owned by Egbert Watt, who had married Grace Frenzel, a schoolteacher from Ilda. According to Howrey, Watt "was trying to eke out a living and support a family on fifty acres of worn-out land. When I offered him $10,000 for his property, he jumped at the chance."[28]

While Howrey details his efforts to become a gentleman farmer in the autobiography, he clearly had a stronger interest in more traditional upper-class pursuits. He devotes thirteen pages of the book to his foxhunting exploits, followed by an anecdote involving his attempt to teach the maid to say "porch" instead of "poach." (The punchline of the story: "From then on, we had 'porched eggs' for breakfast.")

Meanwhile, Ilda was becoming less and less relevant. One indication was the decline of the Ilda Church. With its congregation shrinking as people sought job opportunities elsewhere in the county, the church ultimately could no longer pay its assessments to the Methodist Church. In 1936, the Ilda Church closed its doors, and the building was sold for eight hundred dollars.[29]

Perhaps the Methodists also believed their cause in Ilda was doomed. The Methodist Episcopal Church South had been pushing to outlaw liquor since 1886. In the early 1930s, with Prohibition in full swing, the Ilda Dance Hall was apparently a popular destination—and not just for dancing. On August 24, 1931, the *Washington Post* reported, two soldiers from Fort Myer in Arlington were charged with being drunk and disorderly after they allegedly "got out of a taxi in front of the dance hall and started fighting bystanders." Local residents were prepared for just such an eventuality, as they were able to "repel the invasion with axe handles."[30]

In April 1932, three men were arrested at the dance hall, one for possession and transportation of "ardent spirits" and two for drinking in public.[31] Even local clergy were not immune to the lure of demon rum. In May 1932, Father Patrick Murphy of St. Mary of Sorrows Catholic Church in Fairfax Station was arrested near Ilda with a half gallon of booze in his car. He was fined fifty dollars and sentenced to thirty days in jail, but the jail sentence was suspended.[32]

By that time, Ilda's original residents and their descendants had mostly moved on to other communities and states. On June 3, 1932, two special county commissioners announced that two parcels of land of about one acre each that had been owned by Page Parker when he died without leaving a will would be put up for auction. Another six-acre parcel, partly owned by Page Parker and partly by Moses Parker (who also died without a will), were put up for sale as well.[33]

Housing development and road construction in greater Ilda continued apace, even though it frequently caused consternation among residents and Fairfax County officials. In 1942, the county's board of zoning appeals noted that Little River Turnpike was being widened in the Ilda area, with curbs and gutters added. The road, the board noted, "is becoming an increasingly important major highway, with trucking, cross-country and local buses."[34] Road-widening efforts would continue to be a source of controversy among residents, county officials, and the Virginia Department of Transportation, especially at the corner of Little River Turnpike and Guinea Road.

In 1941, a man named George T. Bennett filed a zoning modification request to build a gas station at the corner. Then he skipped town without leaving a forwarding address, failing to make his scheduled appearance before the board of zoning appeals. But the board made it clear that Bennett's presence wouldn't have made much difference, denying his request "on the grounds that little interest was shown in the case by Mr. Bennett, and that there is very little, if any, need for a Gasoline Filling Station on this site."[35]

War and Peace

World War II came early to Fairfax County, before the United States formally entered the fight. "Of course, we had blackouts at night, sometimes," a resident of the town of Burke, near Ilda, remembered in 2005. "I guess they thought someone was going to bomb us. In Burke, they had a tower[,] and women, my mother included, would spend two or three hours a day looking for airplanes."[36]

The men, meanwhile, went off to theaters of war in Europe, Asia, and Africa, causing an exodus from the county. Some did not return. In August 1944, for example, Pfc. Harry L. Baughman of Ilda was killed in the Allied invasion of Nazi-occupied France.[37] But the war also brought an influx of troops—German prisoners of war. Near the end of the war, a POW camp was set up in Fairfax City, just a few miles west of Ilda. Nearly two hundred prisoners were housed at the complex, and despite concerns about escapes and nefarious activities by the prisoners, almost two hundred families eventually employed them as farm laborers.[38]

Ultimately, the Germans were sent home, and American soldiers returned from military service. In the meantime, the federal government was only getting bigger, especially the military presence at the enormous Pentagon office building. That, combined with housing and education benefits enacted for war veterans, led to burgeoning interest in living in Fairfax County, with its relatively easy access to Washington and nearby military facilities.

At war's end, "the fuse was lit for a significant boom in population," noted Russ Banham in a study of Fairfax County's growth. "Suddenly, job opportunities generated by the federal government's postwar expansion made Washington, D.C., and its outskirts the third-fastest growing region in the country." By 1950, almost 100,000 people made their homes in the county—a 140 percent increase in a decade. In 1953, 90 percent of county workers were employees of the federal government or its contractors.[39]

During the war years and afterward, inequities abounded in the county, and segregation was in full force. A 1942 study concluded, "It is evident that much the same situation exists in 1941–42 that existed in 1929–30 in regard to educational facilities available to the Negroes." The white schools, on the other hand, had improved dramatically. All of them, for example, had transportation services. "The situation is quite the opposite" at Black schools, the study concluded, where more students walked to school than were transported. The longest anyone traveled to get to the Merrifield school was three miles—the approximate distance to Ilda.

In Black schools, the study found, "present conditions are much worse than those that exist in the white elementary schools." The value of individual school buildings ranged from $180,000 for Fairfax High School, the highest figure, to $500 for the Merrifield African American school, the lowest. Merrifield had only 200 books in its library, and that was after adding 88 in 1941. Most white schools had more than 1,000 books, and some had as many as 4,600. Black teachers' salaries "are far below the level of white salaries," the study found.[40]

The heart of Ilda, where the blacksmith shop had been located, was still a collection of small houses and farm buildings. But that would gradually change. In 1949, the Fairfax County Board of Zoning Appeals approved the application of Hilda Hatton to operate a private day and boarding school on property she had purchased. Hatton proposed to use the houses on the two-acre tract she had purchased as classrooms. The board approved her petition for a variance from the zoning regulations for the area, which reserved it as rural residential.[41]

The main building of what came to be called the Benjamin Acres School still exists, although it has been completely renovated. At least one Gibson-Parker descendant believed that the building had originally been Moses Parker's home. But the structure does not appear on an aerial photo of the area taken in 1937, suggesting that it was of later vintage. The photo does show other small houses and buildings in the immediate vicinity that likely date from the nineteenth century. These structures, on land that had been owned by the Gibsons and Parkers, would survive well into the twentieth. But unlike Oak Hill, Wakefield Chapel, and other area landmarks, none of the original buildings in Ilda are standing today.[42]

In 1952, the zoning appeals board approved Hatton's application to build a new building on the property to accommodate the growth of the school.[43] The piece of land that had been home to Ilda's founding families would remain an educational and cultural center well into the twenty-first century. In 1970, Hatton would lease the property to Shirley Boyett, another educator, and it would become the Commonwealth Christian School. Ten years later, the Jewish Community Center of Northern Virginia (known as the JCC) opened on the site. Under an agreement with Fairfax County, the JCC would not destroy what became known as the "white house" at the intersection of Little River Turnpike and Guinea Road, even as the community center's facilities grew around it.

Bedrooms over Businesses

In the early 1950s, houses were welcome in Ilda, but not businesses. In 1951, Sylva Dove petitioned the zoning board to open a restaurant on the south side of Little River Turnpike, about half a mile west of Guinea Road. A board member visited the site and reported that he saw no need for a restaurant at the location: "It is a residential area and it was the policy to locate businesses in congested areas. There are two non-conforming stores in this area, but no other business between Fairfax and Annandale."

Dove was confused. He had owned the property for years (indeed, the surrounding area had come to be called Doveville), and he thought he could use it as he pleased. Not anymore. In the new Fairfax County, he would have to get government approval for any new business endeavor. Dove's application was denied.[44]

It was all part of a tug-of-war between those who wanted to capitalize on the opportunity to serve the county's growing population and those who preferred to see it retain its rural character. The *Fairfax Herald,* ever the conservative voice, opined in 1955 that there was "a fundamental difference of opinion between those who wish to preserve something of the county's former quiet charm and those others who would like nothing better than to see the whole section turned into a vulgar modern bustling housing development thickly dotted with such architectural 'gems' as multiple apartments and shopping centers."[45]

Some people weren't fond of the newcomers to the county, either. "These New Yorkers, Californians and foreigners from the Midwest have taken over our churches," one resident said in 1953. "Their children are pushing our children out of their seats in the schools. They're buying up our choice land and razing some of our historic landmarks. . . . We old Virginians just don't exist any more."[46]

"We were a bedroom community," said Jean Packard, who moved into the Ilda area in 1951 and went on to be elected chairman of the Fairfax County Board of Supervisors, in a 2005 interview. "I'd say that less than 10% of the county had a commercial business at all. And people wanted it that way at that time in the '50s. . . . To them, mixing commercial or store, industrial and residential was to many people who moved out here a symptom of urban blight, and they wanted them separated. They didn't want to have anything to do with it. They didn't want gas stations. They didn't want 7-Elevens."[47]

The fear of commercialization would continue for years. In 1966, an applicant went before the zoning board seeking to build a gas station about 250 feet west of the intersection of Prosperity Avenue and Little River Turnpike. There already was a station on the other side of Prosperity at the turnpike. Local residents were appalled at the idea, saying it would turn the neighborhood into a "gasoline alley." One board member expressed surprise at their reaction, saying he thought "a drive-in restaurant or a restaurant of any kind which could go on the property would be much more offensive than a service station. A service station would not generate traffic or draw traffic from other areas, but would only serve the traffic that is already there."[48]

In time, all of the nightmare scenarios envisioned at the zoning board meeting would come to pass, as the intersection became home to two gas stations and two restaurants. One of the latter, known as Squire Rockwell's, became a local institution before being torn down in the early 2000s to make way for a CVS. The other began life as Gino's Hamburgers, part of a short-lived fast-food chain launched by a group that included Baltimore Colts captain Gino Marchetti. Later, it was turned into a Pizza Hut and then became a Japanese restaurant called Ariake. Next to it is the one remaining gas station, and next to that is a 7-Eleven.

In the early 1960s, as housing developments continued to sprout up, the Ilda name lived on in one development along Guinea Road across the street from where Horace Gibson's and Moses Parker's homes and business had been located. An ad in the *Washington Post* declared that in the "delightful Woods of Ilda," modern ramblers would sit on half-acre forested lots.

In the 1964 edition of the *Citizen's Handbook of Fairfax County*, Carlton C. Massey, county executive, boasted that it was "one of the fastest growing counties in the nation," with a population that topped 317,000. "If you are a new resident," he wrote, "we welcome you and your new neighbors, who are arriving at a rate of one every 15 minutes."[49]

The rapid development was due in large measure to the expansion of roads in Northern Virginia. Fairfax County had at one time both passenger trains and an electric trolley connecting it to Washington, but those services had ended by 1951. So the focus was on more, wider, and better roads. Two major highways would have an outsized impact on development of the area in and around Ilda. The first was the Shirley Highway, which connected the Pentagon with Fairfax County and eventually went farther south. Its first section was completed in 1941, and eventually it would link up with the Capital Beltway, which was built from 1958 to 1966. Among the interchanges in the twenty-two miles of Beltway that were built through Fairfax County were ones at its intersections with Little River Turnpike near Ilda and Arlington Boulevard in Merrifield.

As the area grew, federal officials eyed land near the village of Burke, just down Guinea Road from Ilda, as the site for the construction of a new international airport to supplement the existing Washington National Airport in Arlington. "Fairfax County Tract Chosen for Super Air Terminal," the *Washington Star* reported in June 1951.[50] The feds bought up thousands of acres of farmland and set in motion plans to begin construction.

Local residents were up in arms and launched a massive, co-ordinated effort to block the project. A single committee to voice their opposition wouldn't suffice. Multiple ad hoc groups were formed, apparently under the theory that the longer an organization's name, the greater its effectiveness: the Burke Airport Relocation Committee, Homeowners Opposed to a Jet Airport in Fairfax County, and the Northern Virginia Committee Opposed to a Supplemental Airport at Burke, Virginia.

The battle raged for years, but ultimately the federal Civil Aeronautics Authority was forced to consider other sites. The agency eventually eyed a small community in farther-out Loudoun County, which they called Chantilly. In 1958, its residents were shocked to receive letters informing them that their homes were being condemned to make way for the airport. The Shiloh Baptist Church would have to be razed as well.

Local residents, like those in Burke, mobilized to oppose the airport in their community, which they knew as Willard. They formed a citizens' association, and some hired lawyers. But their concerns were swept aside. In November 1962, Dulles International Airport officially opened.

The difference between Burke and Willard was that the latter was largely, and historically, African American.[51]

The Pain of the Pines

Meanwhile, down Woodburn Road to the northeast of Ilda, development of various kinds proceeded at a rapid and extensive pace. Today, the area is almost completely covered with huge corporate headquarters buildings, shopping centers, a large complex of medical facilities around Fairfax Hospital, and single-family homes, townhouses, and apartment complexes. The buildup was the direct result of county officials' and developers' efforts to transform the county from the bedroom community it had become to accommodate corporate operations as well.

Near the end of Woodburn Road on the southern tip of Merrifield sits Pine Ridge Park, a recreational complex covering nearly forty-three acres. It features three rectangular fields (mostly used for soccer), three baseball/softball diamonds, and a concession stand. Towering lights brightly illuminate night games of various sports leagues. Still, a substantial portion of the park is open grass, and a stand of tall, densely packed pine trees stands watch in the southeast corner.

Across a large gravel parking lot is a community garden, its 160 plots carefully tended by local residents. "Love-Peace-Sunshine" is stenciled on the pink-painted entrance to one of them. Both the playing fields and the garden area are evidence of the county's commitment to serving the recreational desires of residents ranging from vegetable growers to youth soccer players and Little Leaguers—along with their hovering, snack-bearing parents.

"Dedicated to the Citizens of Fairfax County Who Built, Preserved, and Continue to Maintain This Park," reads an inscription on the entrance gate. Nearby, a roadside marker provides information about the history of the area.

It's enough to make one want to congratulate the forward-thinking government officials or benevolent landowners who reserved or donated this much valuable property for recreational use. But neither of those things happened. The real story is summed up in a single sentence in the 2007 master plan for the park approved by the Fairfax County Park Authority: "The land that would become Pine Ridge Park was acquired by Fairfax County Public Schools from private owners in the mid-1960's."[52]

That, however, is far from the full story. Understanding how Pine Ridge Park came into existence requires knowing exactly who those private owners were and how they were connected to the founders of Ilda.

As part of the mini-diaspora of the Gibson-Parker clan to Merrifield, other parts of Fairfax County, and points north, Gladys Parker, daughter of Page and Matilda Parker, married Norman Collins of Merrifield in 1928. Norman was the son of William Collins Jr., who was a member of the famed Buffalo Soldiers who stormed up San Juan Hill alongside Teddy Roosevelt's Rough Riders in the Spanish-American War. After the war, William bought the land where Pine Ridge Park now sits and moved there with his father, William Sr.

It wasn't an expensive purchase, because the land wasn't well-suited to farming. It was thickly covered with pine trees, which the Collinses and other residents painstakingly set about removing. In time, they cleared enough land to start farming. Eventually, other family members also took up residence in what became known as the Pines. Even after much of the area was cleared, "I thought that I was almost in the jungle because it was so woody," Avonjeannette "Dolly" Hill, a family member who moved to the Pines with her parents, remembered years later.

But William Collins Jr. managed to establish a successful farming operation, transporting produce into Washington for sale. He also shared the fruits of his labors with local residents—and not just family members and other African Americans. "He would feed the white people down in the Pines," said Hill. "He made his garden and these people didn't have as much as we had."[53]

"The interesting thing I think about Merrifield and the Pines is that we really had our own; we really took care of each other," said Marion Dobbins, Hill's niece, in a 2008 interview. "If somebody needed, they got. If a family needed, I remember at [First Baptist] church services they would say, 'We're gonna hold a special collection because sister so-and-so needs to buy her medicine.' And everybody would put money in so sister so-and-so could get their medicine; or 'So-and-so needs food,' so we're gonna get you food; or we're gonna get you clothes or whatever."[54]

"Merrifield was a close-knit community, I mean . . . if one was hungry, everybody was hungry. If one ate, everybody ate. You know, they shared," said Aileen Wright, the great-granddaughter of Moses Parker, who grew up there in the 1940s, in 2007.[55]

Along with other families, the Collins clan—including Norman and Gladys—turned the Pines into a vibrant community where their children would grow up, attend the local Black elementary school, and go to Sunday services and social events at the First Baptist Church. Five generations of Collinses lived in the Pines, through the years of Jim Crow and segregation. Even the drive-in movie theater that eventually opened in Merrifield was off-limits to Black residents. Left to their own devices, the children picked apples, played ball, and went sledding down the hill on Woodburn Road in the winter.

In 1964, however, everything changed. That's when five children of William Jr.—Myra, Helen, Elburn, Guy, and Roscoe—received letters from the Fairfax County School Board. We need your land to build a new high school, the letters said. You have 60 days to accept our offer to buy you out and leave, or your property will be condemned.

With no real choice, the Collinses took the offer and left. The wrecking crews arrived almost immediately. Collins family members and their descendants believed their property was targeted because of their race. In a story looking back at the events published in 2000, the *Washington Post* reported that in February 1965, a county official had referred to the Pines as "the colored property." Another memo the next month noted that the site had five homes on it, "none [with] a very high value."[56]

After the houses were razed came—nothing. The school was never built. School board officials had miscalculated where the county's population growth would take off, and its western section would prove to have a more urgent need. So there the Pines sat, empty and unused. In 1975, the community garden was created. Five years later came the athletic fields. The U.S. Naval Reserve Mobile Construction Battalion—better known as the Seabees—pitched in with their heavy equipment to flatten what was left of the Pines to make way for the fields. The total value of the volunteer effort was estimated at $300,000. Both the gardeners and the sports organizations raised money for the creation of the fields and associated facilities and the upkeep of the area.

Despite having concluded there was no need for a school at the Pines, the school board held on to the property—and other parcels of land they had purchased as the need for schools continued to grow—for years. The board leased the Pines to the county's parks authority but kept a tight grip on the land, watching its value grow as development of the area continued steadily. By 1997, the property had an assessed value of $4.2 million. "We have got half a billion dollars in unmet capital needs," the school board chairman said at the time. "Obviously, when we have a property with commercial value, we need to take that into consideration."[57]

"We keep the land because we may need it," another school board official said of the board's general approach to its property holdings three years later. "It makes, I think, remarkably sound business sense. . . . What goes up in value? Land."[58]

Eventually, the Pines was formally transferred to the park authority. The Collins family hired lawyers in an effort to have their property returned, to no avail.

One part of the Pines remains. It's west of the stand of pine trees, down a path a short distance from the playing fields. It's the home of the Sons and Daughters of Liberty Cemetery, the last resting place for several Collins family members and others who lived in the Pines. It's named for an African American service organization that operated for years in Merrifield. For a time, the cemetery fell into disrepair. Wright, her sister, and a cousin were among the small number of people who visited it. "The three of us would be dragging across them fields with flowers, [through] people's gardens and things. [We] climbed the barbed wire fence to get into the cemetery. Every year the three of us, and our children strung along behind us."[59]

By comparison with other African American cemeteries—and for that matter, many old white cemeteries in the county—the Sons and Daughters of Liberty Cemetery is now fairly well-maintained, thanks to the efforts of First Baptist Church members and preservationists. Most of the markers in the quiet, bucolic graveyard are decades old. But one monument is newer. It belongs to a descendant of the Collinses—and, further back, the Gibsons and Parkers—who would come to play a critical role in making sure that the cemetery was preserved and their legacy was not lost. But he wouldn't live to see many of the fruits of his efforts.

Opposite of Itself

The effects of development and population growth that were playing out in Merrifield in the mid-twentieth century were having a similar impact in Ilda. Real estate developers saw what was coming as the federal government grew and closer-in suburbs became more expensive. One of them was a man named Gareth M. Neville.

In the late 1940s, Neville set up a company called Marr Inc., with its principal office in the city of Fairfax, and began buying up land in the county. Neither he nor anyone else associated with the company were named Marr, so it's likely that the name was an homage to John Quincy Marr, the Confederate soldier from Fairfax County said to be the first killed in the Civil War. Marr's name also eventually was attached to a major road running through downtown Annandale.

The development of Annandale and its surrounding areas was kicking into high gear, and Neville seized the opportunity. He eyed a piece of property in Ilda that included the tract that had once belonged to Mary Minor. After her death, it went into trusteeship and then passed into the hands of several owners until it came into the possession of Walter A. Smith in 1946.

In 1950, Neville and his wife, June, purchased the property as part of a tract totaling more than sixty acres. They planned to get in on the postwar trend of packing suburban subdivisions with houses attractive and affordable to the federal workers and military service members flooding into the county. In August 1951, Marr Inc. announced it would begin construction of forty four-bedroom houses on a section of land near the intersection of Little River Turnpike and Guinea Road. The name of the subdivision would be a nod to the Confederate past: Lee Forest.[60]

"Lee Forest is just a breeze away from Washington (and what a breeze to enjoy after the city's heat), yet it's like living in the country," read a Marr Inc. newspaper ad promoting the development. "Plenty of room for the children to run and play and stay outdoors. All of the inside conveniences that Mother could ask for."[61]

The deed of dedication establishing Lee Forest puts more emphasis on outside conveniences, specifically banning them.

"Outdoor toilets and privies are hereby prohibited," it reads. Also, while children were fine outdoors, "no swine shall be kept on any lot in this subdivision."

But it's not just livestock that were excluded from the community. The deed spells it out in bone-chillingly straightforward language: "The land hereby subdivided is made expressly subject to the restriction that no part of said land shall ever be sold or conveyed to any person not of the Caucasian race."[62]

Ilda had, in one clause in a real estate deed, become the opposite of itself. Even though the Supreme Court had ruled in 1948 that governments could not enforce racial covenants, the clause remained on the books. Had the descendants of Ilda's founders wanted to live across the road from the houses and shops their ancestors had built, they would have been expressly forbidden to do so. The Gibsons and Parkers had built a community that housed and served whites and Blacks. They were among the first Americans to seek to truly live out the promise of equality enshrined in the Declaration of Independence. Their business and homes anchored the community. They enjoyed economic success, helped create schools, churches, charitable organizations, and other institutions. They launched a line of descendants who would become successful across Northern Virginia, the United States, and the world.

And now their community was a certified embodiment of white supremacy.

Restrictive covenants like the one in the Lee Forest subdivision were common at the time. But that makes it no less shocking to see one applied to an area that owed its very existence to the vision, business acumen, tenacity, and resilience—to the point of being able to withstand threats of deadly force, a vicious assault, and even a shotgun attack—of its Black founders.

White developers capitalized on the groundwork that had been laid by Horace Gibson and Moses Parker, creating real estate empires. Neville's record appears to be mixed in this regard. Lee Forest developed into a solid community, its small homes lasting for more than fifty years, until newer, wealthier residents tore many of them down and replaced them with more extravagant residences. But in 1956, no fewer than sixteen different lots Neville owned in Lee Forest appeared on Fairfax County's delinquent tax list.[63]

Neville didn't have much more success with commercial development associated with the subdivision. One section of the layout of the Lee Forest subdivision was marked "not included" in the housing development—the corner lot that had been home to Franklin and Mary Minor. According to the deed, that lot was fair game for commercial development of any kind that Neville could get approved. In 1952, he sought to have the property rezoned so he could build a grocery store there, even though there must have been clear indications at that point that there was a graveyard on the site. No grocery store or any other kind of business was ever opened on the lot. But that wasn't for lack of trying.

First there was the 1941 proposal to build a gas station that never got off the ground. Then Neville's effort. After that failed, he sold the property in 1953 to another developer, John C. Webb, who ended up donating it to the Salvation Army. In 1972, the Salvation Army announced plans to build a new Fairfax County headquarters on the site, capable of housing forty children on an emergency basis. The $750,000 building was never constructed. In 1978, a company called Early Learning Centers filed an application to open a day care center on the site, with the support of Salvation Army officials. Local homeowners' associations rallied against the proposal, saying it would cause traffic problems and set a bad precedent for the neighborhood. The application was denied.[64]

In 1983, KinderCare Learning Centers took a shot at establishing a childcare facility at the site but withdrew it. In 1990, a new owner of the property sought to subdivide the lot and build two homes there. Only one was approved, in the approximate location of the Minors' house on the western section of the lot. That house is still there.

The eastern end, on the other hand, has had an almost supernatural resistance to commercial or residential development. Why? Because there was an open secret about the property. Its existence turns up from time to time in official records, such as the minutes of the Fairfax County Planning Commission meeting to consider KinderCare Learning Centers' proposal. One of the presidents of the local civic associations "pointed out that the subject property had been used as a cemetery at one time and that there were still graves on the property."[65]

Neville, for his part, apparently was undeterred by his failure to develop the plot of land and continued to pursue real estate deals. In 1957, he petitioned the board of zoning appeals regarding a forty-acre piece of property he owned south of Ilda, not far from Guinea Road.

He wanted to use it as a cemetery.

5

Determination

IN APRIL 1963, Beryl Dill Kneen, the religious news editor of the *Northern Virginia Sun*, attended services at a new church near the Little River Turnpike–Guinea Road intersection. "As a by-product of my visit to Bethlehem Lutheran, I found out where Ilda is," she reported. "If Ilda is really a place."[1]

Ilda now bore the burden of proof of its own existence.

The following year, a fourteen-year-old African American student named Dennis Howard took his place in a social studies class taught by Mrs. Lois Bouilly at Stratford Junior High School in Arlington, Virginia. Stratford had been the first secondary school in the state to desegregate after the landmark Supreme Court ruling in *Brown v. Board of Education*. But that didn't mean it moved swiftly. Virtually no schools in Virginia did.

At the time of the *Brown* decision in May 1954, there was no public high school for African American children in Fairfax County. Luther Jackson High School didn't open until four months after the decision. Before that, Black students who wanted to continue their education beyond elementary school either had to make their way to Arlington or Washington, or ride a bus to Manassas Industrial School, twenty miles west. The latter required a long, unpleasant trek.

At 7:30 a.m., Black students "had to be at the store in Merrifield to catch the bus," remembered Aileen Wright, one of those students. "And school started at 9:00." The bus had no heat, and the trip necessitated multiple stops to pick up Black students from around Northern Virginia. Their destination was often frigid in the winter as well. "Sometimes you'd get to the school and there wasn't any heat," Wright said. "So we sat on the radiators sometimes—take turns to get a little heat."[2]

After *Brown*, Virginia's elected officials, led by U.S. Senator Harry Byrd, launched a campaign of "massive resistance" to desegregation. "All hell broke loose," said James Keith, a member of the board of supervisors at the time and later its chairman, in a 1974 interview. "He was a terribly strong man and terribly strong politically and had a big following in the state and that's all it took. From then on every step of the way was 'Fight, fight, fight! Sue, sue sue!' And it was a long time before we were integrated."[3]

Private "segregation academies" were set up throughout Virginia, such as the Flint Hill School in Fairfax County. In 1959, the county's school board approved sixty tuition grants for students to attend private schools. Of those, forty-four went to students to enroll at Flint Hill. "It's almost a public school, isn't it?" said board member C. Turner Hudgins.[4]

The same year—a full five years after the Supreme Court declared segregated schools to be unconstitutional—the superintendent of Fairfax County schools was still fighting the legal requirement to integrate classrooms. "The order to desegregate schools is highly improper and infringes on human rights," W. T. Woodson wrote in a 1959 memo. "To force integration of schools . . . is most unfair. It takes advantage of the immaturity of children in that it tends to use it to force upon both parents and children social adjustments to which so many parents strongly object. What part should parents play in choosing their children's associates?"

Woodson also implied that African Americans preferred segregation, writing that people in the United States "generally do not wish to be in social groups where their presence is not generally acceptable."[5]

In 1960, nineteen African American students integrated eight whites-only Fairfax County public schools. But that was just the beginning of a long process. As of 1962, Luther Jackson High School continued to serve virtually all African American students in the county.[6] It wasn't much different in Arlington. So when Dennis Howard took his place in Mrs. Bouilly's classroom in 1964, he was one of only a handful of Black students at Stratford, and the only one in her class.

Howard had grown up in the Tremont Gardens neighborhood of Falls Church, near Merrifield, before moving to Arlington. His maternal grandparents, Sarah and Clarence Gibson, had a farm in Merrifield and were among the deacons and deaconesses of the First Baptist Church. Howard grew to have fond memories of his visits to see them. "I played with all the farm animals, raided all the fruit trees, and drove an old truck on my grandparents' farm," he wrote. "I was sheltered in the Jim Crow South by the love of parents, relatives, and blue-collar segregated communities. I was ignorant and ignorance was bliss."[7]

The Stratford Setup

When Howard got to Mrs. Bouilly's class at Stratford, though, he got a crash course in the realities of race relations.

Mrs. Bouilly was a proper, conservative woman in her sixties who favored A-line flowered dresses. She was an experienced teacher with a firm idea of how her subject should be taught, and

Dennis Howard in a 2006 photo. (Courtesy of John Browne)

she wasn't about to deviate from her lesson plan to suit the new reality of an integrated student body.

The teacher took her place at the head of the class and announced an assignment, one that she had long required of the white students she was accustomed to teaching: trace your family history and bring in a copy of your family crest to share with the class. For Howard, the task would be very difficult, if not impossible. He felt singled out. But he was not the type to back down under such circumstances—and never would be.

"I said, well, this is a setup," he recalled years later. "I can't do that." But then, he said, "I took it as a challenge. I said, 'This lady's not going to bring me in and embarrass me in front of all these students. My pride and my self-respect, my dignity, and my family pride—we're going to do something with this challenge.'"

Howard asked his three living grandparents for help. "I went with pencil and paper in hand, and . . . I said, 'This teacher threw this challenge on me, and, you know, how am I going to handle this?' And so they gave me what they could give me."[8]

It turned out to be quite a lot. His grandmother Sarah could trace her family back to about 1800. She believed that Osborne

Perry Anderson, who rode with John Brown at Harpers Ferry, was an ancestor. Anderson's mother was a white Irish abolitionist.

There it was: not the family crest Mrs. Bouilly had sought but something much more interesting and impressive. Howard became obsessed with tracing his family's history in more detail. It wasn't easy. His maternal grandfather, Clarence Gibson, in particular, wasn't exactly voluble on the subject. "He was the most closed-mouthed of the information-givers," Howard said. "Some of the things I asked him, he told me, 'They don't come before you,' and I didn't know what that was. So I asked my Aunt Ada [Scott], what does that mean? And she said, 'That means it's none of your business.'"[9]

Howard was able to pry one piece of information from his grandfather: that Clarence's grandfather was a formerly enslaved blacksmith named Horace Gibson, who had set up shop in Fairfax County and had become a successful businessman and landowner. Now Howard was even more intrigued, and he was off and running on what would turn into a forty-year quest to document his family's history—and, when he learned how influential his ancestors were, to preserve and protect their legacy.

Howard was born in 1950, so he grew up on the cusp of the civil rights movement, in an era when the entrenched ways of interaction between Black and white residents of Northern Virginia were only beginning to change. He remembered traveling to Washington with his mother and father on special occasions, "paying 10 or 15 cents and riding on the back of that bus." The requirement that they do so was no longer in force, but his parents couldn't break themselves of the habit.

After attending high school in Arlington, Howard went off to Randolph-Macon College in Ashland, Virginia. He was one of the first African Americans to attend the school and became the first to graduate in four years. Howard, who stood six feet, five inches tall and weighed about 250 pounds by the time he was a senior, had been recruited to Randolph-Macon to play basketball. He ended up as the team's captain his senior year. He scored 941 points during his collegiate basketball career—which still ranks him among the school's top fifty scorers of all time—even though he was recruited for his defense and rebounding ability.

Howard also served as a leader in Randolph-Macon's student government association, despite the fact that his political views were at odds with those of many students and professors. "The college was very conservative at that time–very resistant to change," he remembered later. "I had a black militant value system. My heroes were H. Rap Brown, Angela Davis, [and] Bobby Seale." There was, he remembered, "a lot of racial tension. Many times I would have to defend my values by myself."

Sometimes, attending an overwhelmingly white school had its advantages. Howard recalled that once when he was home on a break from his studies, he got a speeding ticket. "And the judge in Arlington County asked, 'What do you do?' And I said, 'Well, I'm a student.' And he asked where did I go to school. I said Randolph-Macon." Howard then made a ripping sound indicating that the judge tore up the ticket.

"And he had to be thinking, 'How does a Black guy go to Randolph-Macon?'"[10]

During Howard's senior year in 1972, three letters from the United States Army arrived at his mother's home in Arlington, informing him that his number had come up in the draft. The letters were progressively more insistent, but Howard didn't see them because he was at Randolph-Macon. The last said he must report to Fort Jackson, South Carolina, in six weeks for basic training. He did, and after that, it was off to Vietnam.

When he completed his active-duty service, Howard entered the Howard University School of Social Work in Washington. Then he embarked on a twenty-one-year career as a child protective services officer for the District of Columbia government.

But Howard also would remain an Army Reserve officer, assigned to a medical unit based in Virginia. This called him away for training and for active-duty deployments. For example, when the United States invaded Iraq in 2003, Howard was called up for service at the Madigan Army Hospital at Fort Lewis, Washington. By the end of his military career, he had risen to the rank of lieutenant colonel and had been awarded the Army Commendation Medal, granted for "conspicuous acts of heroism or meritorious service."

With his basketball build and military bearing, Howard cut an imposing figure. This served him well in his later interactions with government officials. He was never threatening, but he knew his way around a bureaucracy and wasn't above being the squeaky wheel when the situation demanded it. In recorded interviews, he is polite and soft-spoken. But he is insistent in making his points, especially when he believes he is in the right and critical issues are at stake. These personality traits would come in handy when he became involved in a controversy over the cemetery on Guinea Road. He knew well that the default position of many public officials was not to take the concerns of Black citizens seriously, and he was determined to make sure that didn't happen when it came to his family's history.

Joining Forces

Thirty years after delivering his report to Mrs. Bouilly, Howard was still on his quest to fully complete her assignment—talking to relatives, conducting hour after hour of research, and gathering every bit of information he could find about his ancestors. He believed he was plowing fresh ground in that regard.

One day in the early 1990s, Howard got a call from his Aunt Ada, who at that time lived not far from the old Ilda crossroads. "Dennis, come over," she said. "There's someone I want you to meet."

Hareem Badil-Abish. (Courtesy of
Worthie Duckett, estate of Hareem
Badil-Abish)

"Well, who?" he said.

"Jesse Wright," she responded. "He goes by Hareem Badil-Abish now."

"What am I going to meet him for? Just give me some agenda. What am I meeting him about?"

"Well, all of this historical bit that you're doing, he's already done it, and you're duplicating his effort. Why don't you guys go in together?"[11]

Howard and Badil-Abish, it turned out, were related and shared a fierce determination to document and protect their family's history in Fairfax County. Howard was confident that he would impress Badil-Abish with the work he had done, but Badil-Abish actually was much further along in his research. "It was a pleasure and quite a surprise to see how much information you had gathered," Badil-Abish wrote to Howard in 1993. "Although I have the same material and more, it confirms that the material that I have is factual and at least another individual has authenticated my research thus far."[12]

Badil-Abish was in the process of preparing a manuscript for a book based on exhaustive records research and documentation of the family's oral tradition, along with photos and other family memorabilia.

"Hareem and I clicked right away, and discovered we had a mutual love for history," Howard wrote later.[13] The enthusiasm the two shared for their work is palpable. Referring to one Gibson relative as a "wild and crazy guy" who had served time in the Fairfax County Jail for stealing a horse, Badil-Abish wrote in his 1993 letter, "He did not take any crap from the white man!"

Badil-Abish, it turned out, had something of great value that Howard did not—the family records kept by Mollie Bland, an ancestor born in the 1850s. "Aunt Mollie's Journal," as family members called it, was a collection of handwritten notes, newspaper clippings, and obituaries. Badil-Abish used it as the basis for an ever-expanding body of research.

"He would go over to the archives, and he would go to cemeteries and churches and look at death records," Howard said. "He would go to government statistics and look at birth records. He would look at marriage records. He would look at census records, and he knew the whole bit. He studied how to do the research."

Badil-Abish was born in 1952, the son of Aileen (Collins) Wright and Jesse Wright of Merrifield. Aileen was the eldest of two children born to Norman Collins and Gladys (Parker) Collins, the granddaughter of Page Parker and Matilda Gibson.

Badil-Abish grew up in Merrifield and was active in the First Baptist Church at a young age, eventually serving as a Sunday school teacher. The family later moved to Maryland, where he graduated from Central High School.

Badil-Abish enlisted in the U.S. Marines in 1970 and served as an aircraft engineer. He was married while serving in the military and settled in Cleveland with his wife. In 1978, he took a job with Boeing Aircraft Co., and they moved to Iran. There he serviced planes for the country's ruling family until Americans were evacuated from the country. Two years later, they were back in the Middle East, this time in Saudi Arabia, where Badil-Abish worked an eighteen-month stint with Bell Helicopter.

During this period, Badil-Abish began using the name Hareem, meaning "protector of the faithful," and converted to Islam. After he and his wife divorced, he legally changed his name in 1985. After working in Miami and Savannah, Georgia, he moved to New Jersey. There he started his own photography business and threw himself into volunteering with the Court-Appointed Special Advocate (CASA) program, serving as a representative in the legal process for children who have suffered abuse or neglect. In 1993, he was named CASA volunteer of the year. The following year he married again, this time to ThomaSena Culbertson. They would have two sons, in addition to the daughter he had from his previous marriage.[14]

Throughout all of this, Badil-Abish pursued his passion, which was his family's history. The manuscript of his book grew larger and larger. "My initial intent was to write the history of my family in Merrifield, Virginia," he wrote in an author's note. Now he hoped to broaden the scope of his work. "It is my hope and desire to continue documenting and bringing forth the true history of the various Black communities and their contributions made in the development of the Northern Virginia society and Fairfax County in particular."

Badil-Abish's work meticulously chronicling the Gibson-Parker family history ultimately would serve as the backbone of in-depth research and analysis of Ilda and the Guinea Road Cemetery, yielding results that would surprise county officials and family members in very different ways.

White Flag and Whitewash

Dennis Howard and Hareem Badil-Abish grew up in an era when segregation had nominally come to an end in Northern Virginia.

Many white residents thought the integration process was over and had gone quite smoothly.

"I don't remember any trouble" when the process finally got started in Fairfax County, said James Keith. "We integrated so easily you wouldn't have known it." He acknowledged, though, that the "real segregationists" ended up sending their children to private schools.[15]

Although Fairfax County didn't have to call out the National Guard to integrate its schools, the process took a long time. The Fairfax Education Association, representing teachers, didn't change a provision in its regulations that membership was open to "any white person engaged in the public schools of Fairfax County" until late 1962.[16]

An even bigger issue than who was doing the instructing was what they were teaching. Because in that regard, the Lost Cause effect was still very much in force.

In 1966, the county government distributed a booklet to schools titled *A County Called Fairfax: Being a Student's Digest of Our Government and History*. It contained a section titled "The War for Southern Independence" that presented the story of "a Virginia County occupied by the Union troops throughout the conflict and the bravery of many men who fought for the Stars and Bars."

The fact that it was not the Stars and Bars, but a white flag of surrender, that Confederate forces waved to end the war did not dissuade the pamphlet's authors. In fact, they painted a picture of a vanquished army's laudable and magnanimous decision to stop fighting. "From Appomattox a proud Army marched into history," they wrote. "To many this may have been Virginia's proudest hour. It preserved a nation undivided."[17]

The word "slavery" does not appear in the brief history.

Likewise, the textbooks that were required reading in schools throughout Virginia contained racist descriptions of African Americans and fantastical characterizations of plantation life.

Garrett Epps described the books in an October 2021 article in *Washington Monthly*.[18] One of them, *Virginia: History, Government, Geography,* declared that slavery "made it possible for the Negroes to come to America and make contacts with civilized life" in a place "far away from the spears and war clubs of enemy tribes" in Africa. Plantations were "happy and prosperous," and "all slaves were given medical care."

Cavalier Commonwealth: History and Government of Virginia taught students that Virginia's slaveholders "regarded themselves as benefactors of a backward race," and "indeed in some respects they obviously were." Slaves were given "plentiful food . . . warm cabins, leisure and free health care."

A Hornbook of Virginia History summed it up: "The debt the Negro race owes to Virginia and the South has never been less recognized than it is today. Virginia took a backward race of savages, part cannibal, civilized it, [and] developed many of its best qualities."

These were not nineteenth-, or even early twentieth-century texts, and they were not written by fringe groups. They were state-sanctioned teaching materials, and they weren't officially withdrawn from use in schools until 1972.

Even historians who were becoming aware of the importance of telling Black stories weren't sure how to do it, and they often lacked access to documents that would help them. In the summer of 1977, the year that Alex Haley's *Roots* became a nationwide phenomenon, a historic preservation newsletter produced by the Fairfax County Office of Comprehensive Planning reported that records of the registrations of free African Americans in the county, which had been presumed lost, had been uncovered. In the absence of such records, oral tradition was greeted with skepticism. That was problematic because, in many instances, it was the only way that African American history was remembered.

Even with the best of intentions, efforts to integrate stories of the African American experience into the presentation of the county's history were very slow to develop. That, in turn, meant that historic preservation efforts rarely focused on the Black experience. This left it up to people like Dennis Howard and Hareem Badil-Abish to do the necessary research to tell Black stories independently and to cajole public officials into protecting the legacy of African American residents.

Badil-Abish, for example, was appalled at the condition of the Sons and Daughters of Liberty Cemetery. In 1907, the lodge bought the quarter-acre parcel of land on which the cemetery sits, because the deed to the First Baptist Church didn't allow a cemetery to be placed on the property. The cemetery was condemned in 1965 along with other properties in the Pines and turned over to the Fairfax County School Board for the high school that was never built.

"The cemetery was not maintained and suffered severely from neglect and vandalism," according to a county cemetery inventory.[19] At the prodding of Badil-Abish and others, in 1990, the school board began to clear the cemetery of underbrush, fence it off, and identify graves. Only one original gravestone survives. Others were replaced in a process that was completed by May 1993. Since that time, volunteers have periodically cleaned up and maintained the cemetery.

Uncomfortable Mix

On a winter day in 1971, future board of supervisors chairman Sharon Bulova, her husband, and their young son set off on a house-hunting expedition in Fairfax County. Their trek quickly took them off the beaten path in a way that reflected the state of development in the region.

"After winding through trees and over muddy terrain," she later wrote, "the dirt road opened up onto broad pavement. On one side of the road were Patty's Riding School and an old farmhouse. On the other side stretched a newly minted subdivision of brick and frame houses." They weren't sure exactly where they were until they saw a map in a model home in the Kings Park West development. The dirt road they had been following was a yet-to-be upgraded section of Guinea Road, a couple of miles from Ilda.[20]

Even in the immediate Ilda area, Guinea remained an unpaved, narrow, two-lane road until the 1960s. It wasn't widened until the early 1970s. Until then, its nickname, according to a local resident at the time, was "Skinny Guinea."[21]

Fairfax County was an ever more uncomfortable mix of the rural, the suburban, and, increasingly, commercial development of its own. By 1971, the county's population had grown to nearly 470,000 people. It jumped to 515,000 the following year. Subdivisions like the one that caught the eye of the Bulovas continued to sprout like weeds, and now major corporations had begun to eye the region, too. Its high quality of life and proximity to policymakers in Washington made it a tempting home for big companies. At this time, about 60 percent of all development in the Washington metro area was occurring in Fairfax County.[22]

For residents of the county, though, enough was enough. The old school of Virginians were already fed up with what they viewed as an attack on their way of life. And many newcomers were eager to see the door closed to further expansion. As usual, roads were a fulcrum in the debate.

The same year that the Bulovas purchased their home in Kings Park West, the entire nine-member board of supervisors came up for reelection. A slate of slow-growth and no-growth candidates were swept into office. The following year Jean Packard, an environmental and antidevelopment activist, was elected chairman of the board.

Packard insisted she and the new board members favored managed growth, not a halt to development. "Growth was fueled by new roads," she later said. Controlling their spread theoretically would put the brakes on runaway development. "We had the power to do it," Packard said. "We knew [the Virginia Department of Transportation] wouldn't build a road if the local jurisdiction was against it."[23]

The only problem with this approach was that people kept moving into the county, and developers went ahead and developed anyway. They viewed transportation as the county's problem. This put increasing pressure on the existing road system and started an endless cycle in which roads stayed several steps behind population growth and the pace of construction in both residential and commercial districts. This would continue to play out well into the twenty-first century.

While politicians struggled to respond to pressure to control growth, Fairfax County's bureaucratic machinery continued to promote it in various ways. Minority communities lacking the political clout to counter such efforts were particularly affected. In the early 1970s, for example, the county's Economic Development Authority voted to expand an obscure entity known as the Washington Commercial Truck Zone, doubling the size of the area in which commercial truck deliveries were allowed. The move would have a dramatic impact on industrial development in Merrifield, which was later described as a "dilapidated assortment of rundown dwellings, businesses and unused land." It was transformed into a "fast-growing, unified industrial and business complex with more than 130 firms employing over 3,000 people."[24]

The board of supervisors' attempt to pump the brakes on growth was short-lived. In 1975, when Packard came up for reelection, she was defeated by Jack Herrity, the lone Republican

Little River Turnpike near the Guinea Road intersection in the 1970s.
(Photo by Jim Tingstrum; courtesy of Fairfax County Public Library)

on the board and a vocal advocate for untrammeled growth. In fact, he said there was no point in trying to stop it, because it was as "uncontrollable as the weather."[25]

So, in the years that followed, the county's growth in population, housing development, and commercial construction would continue in largely uncontrolled fashion. In 1955, there was just a single office building in the entire county, with fewer than 6,000 square feet of space. By 1971, there were almost 150 commercial buildings containing nearly 5 million square feet of space. And that was just the beginning.[26]

The boom that followed brought millions more square feet of offices and a wide range of companies. In 1980, Mobil Corp. brought its marketing and refining divisions to the county. Nine years later, the company would relocate its global headquarters to a massive complex in Merrifield. (The dirt from that construction project was dumped in the area formerly known as the Pines.) Mobil became the largest business in the greater Washington area by a wide margin.

Determination

In the process of growth, Fairfax County became less diverse. Families like those who had left Ilda for Merrifield in turn left Merrifield for farther-out suburbs or other states. In 1970, 93 percent of the county's population was white, and only 3.5 percent was African American—down from more than 5 percent a decade earlier. Gradually, the percentage of Black residents then began creeping back up again, reaching 6 percent by 1980.

All of these changes were felt in what was left of Ilda. In 1979, the Commonwealth Christian School at the corner of Little River Turnpike and Guinea Road ran into financial trouble. Parents of students scrambled to raise funds to pay off its $400,000 debt and keep its doors open, but they fell short, and the school closed. What happened next, though, breathed new life into the community.[27]

Starting in 1969, Jewish leaders in Fairfax County had begun discussing the need for a Jewish community center. A decade later, they decided that the time had come to move forward.

Their timing coincided with the closure of the Commonwealth Christian School. The backers of the Jewish community center plan snapped up the property. In May 1980, the Jewish Community Center of Northern Virginia (JCC) opened its doors in the white building at the center of the property. The JCC began purchasing adjacent plots of land with an eye toward creating a larger, permanent structure. They undertook a fundraising effort in 1985 and in December 1990 held a grand opening for the new complex. Then Virginia governor Douglas Wilder was among the attendees.[28]

In the decades that followed, the JCC would become a fixture of the community, serving residents with a gym, a day care center, and cultural events. But the facility would also become a target of the same hate and prejudice that plagued the founders of Ilda.

On the morning of December 1, 1993, members of the community center arrived at the facility to discover that it had been defaced with twenty spray-painted swastikas. One terrifying message scrawled on a wall read, "6 million more." Above it, at the place where Horace Gibson and Moses Parker had started their business, built their homes, raised their families, and forged their legacy, were two crudely and cruelly painted words: WHITE POWER.[29]

A week later, more than one thousand people, including both members of the center and local residents, gathered in solidarity at the center. They heard from then president Bill Clinton in the form of a letter to the Jewish community, which said the vandalism was "an affront . . . to all Americans. I share your outrage at those who would demean the memory of the Holocaust by seeking to intimidate those who carry on their legacy."

In the middle of the gathering, two bomb threats were phoned in to the facility, minutes apart. The callers succeeded only in shifting the meeting outdoors into the wintry night, where Tom Davis, then chairman of the county board of supervisors, said, "It's going to take a lot more than bomb threats to stop us."[30]

End of the Century

By the late twentieth century, Fairfax County had fully transformed. The continued growth of the federal government and, more importantly, its contract workforce, meant that population increases and economic development continued at steady hum. Throughout the latter half of the century, federal employment remained fairly steady, but its reliance on contractors, especially in the information technology arena, increased exponentially. Many of those firms, big and small, built their businesses in or relocated them to Fairfax County.

And while denizens of the District of Columbia and the metro area's inner-ring suburbs still viewed the county as a distant suburb, its leaders were eager to tout its growing cosmopolitan nature.

In 1978, a history of Fairfax County published under the auspices of the county government declared that it was "one of the most affluent political jurisdictions in the world, whose citizens have an extremely high level of academic achievement."

"The higher per capita income in the county is reflected in the lifestyles and numerous material possessions of its residents," the history book continued. "Bridge, canasta, poker, cribbage, and other card games are popular, as well as Monopoly and other board games; ping-pong, billiards, mah jong and sex all have their devotees."

When they weren't playing bridge or having sex, county residents were on the road. "An average of seven to fourteen trips per day are made in motor vehicles in and out of private driveways," the book reported, "taking Fairfax Countians to work, to shop, to educational, recreational, and travel experiences. The private automobile is important; public transportation is inadequate."[31] The Metrorail system in the Washington area had arrived in 1976, but it was in its infancy and was focused on commuters going to and from office buildings in the District of Columbia every day.

Increasingly, this was not the case. In the 1960s, less than a third of people who lived in Fairfax County also worked there. By the 1970s, more than half did so. People were driving not just to Washington, but to Fairfax City, Merrifield, and the burgeoning area of Tysons Corner, which would eventually develop into an "edge city."

And the people kept coming. By 1990, the county's population was nearly 820,000. It was bigger than that of seven states—Alaska, Delaware, Montana, North Dakota, South Dakota, Vermont, and Wyoming.

The pressure on the road system was enormous and constant. At a June 1983 hearing of the Fairfax County Planning Commission, Bernhard Larsen, executive vice president of the Rutherford Civic Association, representing more than six hundred households just south of the Little River Turnpike–Guinea Road intersection, testified about traffic in the area:

Traffic flow for miles around is nothing short of ghastly in peak periods, and growing worse. Main roads are a disaster, their capacity grossly exceeded. Residential streets are rendered a dangerous terror by motorists frantically seeking a way around each day's fresh obstacles. In the past ten years, Guinea Road has gone from a relatively quiet thoroughfare to side-by-side bumper-to-bumper traffic, as the rapidly burgeoning residential and business to the south and to the north and to the west discharge ever growing volumes of vehicles into our road net, which is most emphatically *not* growing.[32]

A decade later, the "Dr. Gridlock" columnist at the *Washington Post* (yes, traffic had become such a headache that the paper had a regular column solely focused on commuter concerns) reported the results of an informal poll he had launched on the longest traffic lights in the Washington metro area, including the Northern Virginia and Maryland suburbs. On the short list was the intersection of Little River Turnpike and Guinea Road.[33] In 2001, the *Post* used the intersection as an example of the type of suburban crossroads that had become so clogged with traffic that its lampposts and telephone poles were littered with advertising aimed at drivers hopelessly stuck in traffic.[34]

To the extent that anyone cared at all about the area that had once been at the center of Ilda, this was what they were concerned about: moving traffic through it in the most efficient way possible. The action in the county and the region was elsewhere. By that time, several iterations of the county's comprehensive plan had called for widening Little River Turnpike from four lanes to six. Indeed, when the Jewish Community Center of Northern Virginia applied for routine adjustments to its zoning status as it expanded, the agreements always included this boiler-plate language relative to the old "white house" on the property: "The smaller two-story structure may remain on the site only until such time as Route 236 is widened to 6 lanes, at which time the applicant shall be responsible for removing this structure and landscaping the resultant area."

Likewise, commuters were increasingly vocal about their frustration with the Guinea Road–Little River Turnpike intersection. Drivers attempting to make a right turn from the turnpike onto Guinea often had to wait for an opening amid the traffic, causing lengthy backups. They were taking their case to county officials, loudly. But their voices were being countered by those of local residents like Larsen carrying on a latter-day variation on the theme that the county was losing its character—this time as a bedroom community. The owners of the homes that had sprouted in the development bonanza starting in the 1950s were already fed up with the heavy flow of cars in their neighborhoods. The last thing they wanted was to encourage more and faster-moving traffic. But developers sought out every nook and cranny among the existing subdivisions to build newer, much bigger houses that presupposed owners who would move in with multiple vehicles.

As the twentieth century came to a close, Fairfax County was aggressively seeking to expand and upgrade its road network, local commuters were tearing their hair out, and residents were becoming increasingly concerned and vocal about the effects of expanding the major arteries cutting through their neighborhoods. At the same time, Hareem Badil-Abish and Dennis Howard's family history research was pointing them in the direction of a place called Ilda. Push was about to come to shove at Little River Turnpike and Guinea Road.

6

Revelation

IN AUGUST 1988, Brian Conley was doing what he loved: tromping around a plot of land in Fairfax County that purportedly contained a cemetery. This particular plot was at the southwest corner of the Little River Turnpike–Guinea Road intersection.

As he drove up to the site, Conley's bookish, beard-and-glasses appearance made him appear not as an intrepid explorer but as what he was: an information specialist in the Virginia Room at the City of Fairfax Regional Library, where he helped manage its voluminous trove of records and reference materials. But then Conley parked his car, donned an Australian bush hat, and unloaded two tools: a machete to clear the thick underbrush and a long metal pole to probe for grave depressions. He was transformed—a little, anyway.[1]

Conley thoroughly assessed the site, looking for any surface indication of graves and probing with the pole for any telltale signs. When he was finished, he filed a report on what he found, one of hundreds he would complete in the process of compiling an inventory of the county's cemeteries. Under the heading

"Unnamed Cemetery," he wrote: "There are two fieldstone markers and three grave-sized depressions in evidence. Site is unkempt and completely overgrown. No inscriptions." Cemetery No. 259 was duly registered on the inventory and recorded as archaeological site 44FX1664.

A year later, Susan Henry of the Heritage Resources Branch of the Fairfax County Office of Comprehensive Planning filed an archaeological report on the site based on Conley's findings. Under "Remarks and Recommendations," it said, "Preserve and maintain."[2]

Explorers of the Suburban Landscape

Conley was among a small group of people who were concerned about preserving the county's numerous small cemeteries, many of which had already given way to development and road construction. His supervisor would later characterize him as "an explorer of the suburban landscape, documenting the history of this community with clues that were left behind by the dead and those who buried them."[3]

Conley also was a master researcher. And he was about to become involved in one of the most convoluted, controversial, and confounding research efforts of his career.

A year after Conley's mini-expedition, William Adams, a developer and real estate agent with Empire Realty in Annandale, went to the site to do some fieldwork of his own. He walked the area and conducted what an archaeologist would later characterize as "subsurficial testing."[4] In the process, he found one of the markers that Conley had identified. Adams removed it and took it with him.

Conley and Adams weren't the only ones who found evidence of a cemetery on the site; nor were they the first. Local residents and their children, lured by the attraction of a mysterious vacant lot that had evaded development for decades, had seen signs, too.

In the mid-1970s, Henry A. Minor and his friend Donald Schudel had explored the property looking for graves. They were residents of the Truro neighborhood just to the east of Guinea Road, near Little River Turnpike. Minor (no relation to the notorious Franklin) was born in 1930 and grew up in the African American section of the town of Vienna in Fairfax County, near Merrifield. He had strong ties to the area's Black community.

Minor had a lengthy career working in the civilian federal government. In 1968, he was elected to a seat on the Fairfax City Council, becoming the first African American to win elective office in the county since Reconstruction. (His victory celebration took place at the Mosby Building across the street from Jermantown Cemetery, where Horace and Martha Gibson and several of their children lay at rest.)[5]

Minor believed, based on conversations with other local residents, that there was a cemetery next to Guinea Road at the Little River Turnpike intersection, and that it contained the graves of African Americans who had once lived in the area. That was enough to pique Schudel's curiosity, and the two set off on a neighborhood expedition.

Sure enough, when they made their way through the wooded area, Minor and Schudel, then a teacher in the Fairfax County school system, discovered three to five dark stones, measuring about 18″ × 12″ × 12″, separated from each other. Minor, who had visited the site when he was younger, remembered there being more grave markers but couldn't find them.[6]

Schudel later explored the site again, around the time that KinderCare Learning Centers attempted to build a day care center there in 1983. This time he brought along his children. They were assessing the location as a possible candidate for a Girl Scout restoration project. He looked for the stones he had seen before, but they had disappeared.

"They were big stones," he later said. "Stones don't walk."[7]

Years later, in a recap of a construction project at Little River Turnpike and Guinea Road, a state official would note, "Citizens from the neighborhood were very interested in what was happening at this busy intersection. Many brought cameras and told tales of how they remembered playing in the woods at this site and they remembered the rocks that were used as headstones."[8]

On July 11, 1983, KinderCare was scheduled to appear before a hearing of the board of supervisors on its request for a special exemption from zoning regulations to build the day care facility. Instead, they sent a letter withdrawing their petition. "The board noted at its hearing that the application had been withdrawn due to the presence of graves on the site," the zoning evaluation office would later report. Board members ordered that county records be marked to indicate that at least five graves were located on the property.[9]

Around this time, John Whitmer headed up the Map Department of the Fairfax County Office of Tax Administration. The possibility that there were unmarked graves at the Guinea Road site came to his attention when the Salvation Army owned the property and was attempting to get it rezoned. Whitmer began investigating. He questioned residents of the neighborhood surrounding the site, some of whom told him that they had heard there were graves on the parcel. He searched the area with a metal detector. He didn't get conclusive results, although he thought that some of the readings might have indicated the presence of old nails. Whitmer concluded the property might contain graves.[10]

By 1990, a long list of attempts to develop the site had failed, to a greater or lesser extent because of a consistent belief among residents that there was a cemetery there. In some cases, that belief was based on firsthand observations. Still, developer Farhang Asgari of Mondan General Contractors was undaunted. He undertook to build two houses on the site.

Asgari, aware that the consensus was that there were graves on the property, was no doubt concerned about disturbing a burial ground—which was illegal under state law. So he hired Kay McCarron, a contract archaeologist, to study the site and report on what she found. In a month's time, she did historical research, conducted a walking survey of the site, and wrote her report.

For the survey, McCarron contacted William Adams, the realtor, who brought along the stone he had taken from the site previously. The two put it back "as near its original position as he could remember," according to her report.[11] They then walked the site, stopping at eight-foot intervals to check for fieldstones, depressions, or mounds. They found a second stone (as had Conley) and a "rectangular depression." McCarron included a description of Whitmer's work in an appendix to her report, including the fact that he thought graves might exist on the property and his belief that "any purchaser should be required to acknowledge in writing" receiving the information that the site may contain graves.

Still, McCarron concluded there was "no evidence of a graveyard" at the site. The fieldstones, she reported, were "in fact nineteenth century boundary markers and not the gravestones which they had been rumored to be." The proof, she said, was twofold: historic deeds didn't mention a cemetery on the property, and "no graveyard is indicated on any plat or map of the area prior to 1980."

Grave Conclusions

With McCarron's report in hand, Asgari went ahead with plans to appeal to the county for a rezoning of the site to allow the erection of two single-family homes. The Fairfax County Planning Commission scheduled a public hearing on his application for December 5, 1990. This caused Brian Conley to get in touch with someone he knew who had family ties to the community where the cemetery was located: Hareem Badil-Abish.

Badil-Abish had contacted Conley in the late 1980s as he was pursuing his family history research effort. He told Conley that he had family documents showing that six members of the Gibson and Parker families were buried at a long-lost cemetery at Guinea Road and Little River Turnpike. Conley was unable to verify the specific burial information Badil-Abish provided, but the details he shared on the parentage, dates of death, and other aspects of the people said to be buried there checked out.

Family tradition, according to Badil-Abish, held that after the founding of Ilda, Mary Minor had allowed the Gibson and Parker families to bury their dead on her property. At first blush, this seems unlikely. After all, Franklin Minor had violent clashes with Horace Gibson from virtually the moment he and Mary arrived in the area. A later analysis would conclude that "it is unlikely that Minor, a lawyer, would have countenanced occasional burial ceremonies in his backyard."[12] But it was actually Mary's backyard. And the fact that she, not he, solely owned the land, may indicate that she had decision-making authority over it. And if the cemetery was a known resting place for African Americans in the area, she may have been inclined to allow the tradition to continue.[13]

On November 14, Conley wrote a letter to Badil-Abish saying he had been contacted by the Fairfax County Office of Zoning Evaluation about the cemetery. "I am giving the information regarding Parker and Gibson burials that you gave me to them," he wrote. "It seems that someone wants to build single-family homes on the site and claims that there is no cemetery on the site." He suggested Badil-Abish get in touch with county officials about the proposal. "Since you are a descendant of the family, your opinion carries a lot of weight."[14]

The same day Conley sent his letter, Larry Moore, a historian with the Environmental and Heritage Resources Branch of

Fairfax County's Office of Comprehensive Planning, sent a memo to Kris Abrahamson of the county's Zoning Evaluation Division. "There is a cemetery" on the Guinea Road lot, he wrote, noting that Conley's work showed the presence of at least five burials. "More graves may be there," he added. "The cemetery should be preserved and a buffer of at least 25 feet around it. Open space." The memo closed by noting that "STATE CODE 18.2–127 states that injury to a cemetery is a Class 6 Felony."[15]

A week later, the staff of the Zoning Evaluation Division recommended that the developer's application to rezone the lot for single-family detached residential units be denied. Their report is more specific about the nature of the cemetery, presumably because of the information Badil-Abish had supplied. The report characterized the graveyard as a "historic Black family cemetery" containing "five to six known graves, dating from approximately 1887 to 1891." The staff recommended that a "thorough survey to delineate the boundaries of the cemetery" be performed and submitted to the county archaeologist for review.

"Although physical evidence has not proven that graves exist in this location to date," the report stated, "there is a significant amount of circumstantial evidence to support the existence of a number of graves."[16]

Asgari didn't give up on his plan, and questions lingered about the lack of concrete evidence of a cemetery. It was time to bring in the big guns.

Star Archaeologist

There aren't actually any Indiana Jones types in the real world of archaeology and anthropology, but there are stars. And Douglas Owsley is one of them. It's not every archaeologist or anthropologist whose Wikipedia page runs to nearly thirteen thousand words and includes nuggets of information like this: His biography, *No Bone Unturned: Inside the World of a Top Forensic Scientist and His Work on America's Most Notorious Crimes and Disasters,* was the basis of a Discovery Channel documentary entitled *Skeleton Clues* and an ABC News 20/20 segment entitled *Murders, Mysteries, History Revealed in Bones,* and he was featured in the film *Nightmare in Jamestown,* produced by National Geographic.

Over the course of his career, Owsley, the curator of biological anthropology at the Smithsonian's National Museum of Natural History, would handle numerous high-profile cases. These included identifying serial killer Jeffrey Dahmer's first victim, excavating the Jamestown Colony, analyzing victims of the siege at the Branch Davidian compound in Texas, and processing remains of U.S. servicemen killed during Operation Desert Storm.

After starting his career in academia, Owsley joined the Smithsonian in 1987 and in 1991 was working in its physical anthropology division. He was well on his way to becoming one of the world's leading experts in the search for and identification of human remains.

In mid-1991, the Heritage Resources Branch asked Owsley to examine the Guinea Road plot of land. On June 19, he set out with Larry Moore, who was by then the county archaeologist, and Malcolm Richardson, a member of the Archaeological Society of Virginia. By the time they visited the site, much of the underbrush had been cleared. The lot now served as a dumping ground for surplus dirt, building materials, and trash.

Owsley, with the help of Richardson, meticulously examined the plot of land. He immediately noticed one white quartz stone marker and several shallow depressions. After extensively probing the ground with half-inch stainless steel rods, they found a total of six graves, all oriented in an east-west direction. Not only that, the probes located stones beneath the surface of the ground marking each grave. Three burial shafts indicated the presence of adult burials. The other three were much smaller, presumably for children.[17]

On July 19, Moore delivered the news to Asgari in a letter. "The number and size of the burials," he wrote, "indicates that Brian Conley's initial historical research was correct." Moore also filled Asgari in on the responsibilities of whoever might end up owning the property: "In brief, the landowner is responsible for maintaining the cemetery. A court order is needed to remove the remains." The Smithsonian, he said, "might be interested in doing this archaeologically because of the potential research value of the remains."

Asgari gave up on his plan to erect two houses on the site—which the zoning board's staff had indicated would be problematic even without the presence of a cemetery, due to the relatively small size of the lot. Only one house was built, in 1993. The home, one of the largest in the neighborhood, sits in the approximate location of Franklin and Mary Minor's house.

This might have been the end of the Guinea Road Cemetery controversy. The owner of the new house didn't disturb the parcel of land that included human remains, out of respect for the dead and their descendants. But another entity had an interest in the land: the Virginia Department of Transportation (VDOT). Traffic snarls at the corner of Little River Turnpike and Guinea Road were getting worse and worse. VDOT and Fairfax County were facing a steady drumbeat of pressure to do something about it.

"A Little Freaky"

"Hello, it's been quite a long time," Hareem Badil-Abish wrote to Brian Conley on March 23, 1995. "The reason I am contacting you is that some time ago, we discussed the burial ground at the corner of Guinea Road and L.R. Turnpike. I stated before that my family had owned that property and several members were buried there. . . . In addition, I have talked to Scott Brown of the Jewish Community Center regarding the family home that is still standing there. I am trying to get the historical society to look into its preservation versus its destruction for the new highway. Any suggestions?"[18]

Based on family oral tradition and his own investigation, Badil-Abish was certain of three things about the cemetery: it sat on land once owned by Horace Gibson; Gibson-Parker descendants were buried there; and the building across Little River Turnpike to the north was Moses Parker's home. All of those conclusions would be disputed or disproven in the years to come. The cemetery had yet to give up its secrets.

Conley wrote back to Badil-Abish the same day he received the letter, sending his updated report on the cemetery, and the county archaeologist's assessment of its existence that took place during the housing development process. "I am looking forward to seeing your research published," Conley wrote. "I know it will be of great benefit and interest to many people."[19]

Conley would eventually see Badil-Abish's work published and included on the reference shelves of the Virginia Room. Badil-Abish, though, would not live to see that happen. He died on November 19, 1997, at the age of forty-five.

Badil-Abish's memorial marker stands out at the Sons and Daughters of Liberty Cemetery in Merrifield. For starters, it's much newer than almost all of the other markers in the graveyard. And it sits alone and apart, on the left near the front gate.

The cemetery, easily accessible after a short walk from the parking lot and past the athletic fields of Pine Ridge Park, isn't in quite as nice of a condition as when it was first restored due to the efforts of Badil-Abish and others. But, for the most part, it is well-maintained. Every year, the graves of military veterans—dating back to the Civil War—are decorated on Memorial Day.

Badil-Abish's marker provides a link between the present and the past. And it seems fitting that it is among those of other, more distant relatives whose stories he was so keen on recording for posterity.

After Badil-Abish's death, Dennis Howard viewed it as his responsibility to complete his work. "I visited him on his deathbed at Veterans Hospital in East Orange, New Jersey, and made a commitment to finish the book," he wrote later. Howard started at the top of the Virginia government. "I am writing to you to request information on my great, great maternal grandfather, Horace Gibson," reads an April 21, 2000, letter from Howard to then Virginia governor James Gilmore III. "Can you refer this matter to someone who can help? I am planning a family reunion for August 2000 and would love to present the finding of this search."[20]

The someone who could provide assistance, Gilmore's staff told Howard, was Brian Conley. "I appreciate any help you can give me and look forward to calling and coming by in the near future," Howard told Conley on May 8.[21] At this point his interest was only in continuing the work he had started at Stratford Junior High in 1964. That would soon change.

In 2004, the Virginia Department of Transportation embarked on a road-widening project that involved several roads that intersected with Little River Turnpike. One of them was Guinea Road. The plan was to create an additional right-turn lane on Guinea and relocate the existing sidewalk at the western edge of the roadway. This, it was hoped, would help alleviate traffic backups at the intersection.

By now, the existence of the cemetery was common knowledge. "It was a little freaky" learning about it, said Maheen Nasim, who lived in the house that now stood on the site. "But we don't think about it that much."[22]

At that time, Andy Williams was the Virginia Department of Transportation's project administrator for the road-widening effort. He knew about the cemetery and was clearly a little freaked out himself. Williams consulted with Conley about the history of the intersection and the families whose ancestors were said to be buried there. He became concerned that the road project, which would affect both the turnpike and Guinea Road, might disturb human remains.

Ordinarily, in the course of such projects, if there were such concerns, VDOT would post a small typed notice on an 8½" × 11" sheet of paper asking if anyone had any information about the site. Williams, in a decision that would have a dramatic impact on the ensuing course of events, took a more aggressive approach. In March 2004, he put up a huge metal sign on a pole driven into the grass near the Guinea Road–Little River Turnpike intersection. "PUBLIC NOTICE," it read. "IF YOU HAVE ANY KNOWLEDGE OF ANYONE BURIED AT THIS SITE OR THEIR DESCENDANTS, PLEASE CALL 703-383-2281."

"I felt like, 'Let's try something different,'" said Williams. "Let's put up a sign people can read."[23] The impossible-to-miss notice attracted the attention of *Washington Post* columnist John Kelly, who would write a series of articles about the intersection and the cemetery over the next several years. The sign also did not escape the notice of commuters and local residents, who tended to have opposite—and strongly held—points of view on the road-widening project.

"I guess that's why somebody stole it," said Williams. The sign disappeared in early April.[24]

With the prominence of the notice and Kelly's articles, information came pouring in from several potential descendants of people who may have been buried at the site.[25] In addition, when Williams learned about Badil-Abish and Howard's research, and the former's death, he tried to call Howard. But he didn't realize that the U.S. Army reservist was at Fort Lewis in Washington State on a deployment. Eventually, Williams sent a letter to

Howard informing him of the road-widening project. In the letter, he said he hoped that Howard, as a "descendant of those buried in the Gibson/Parker Family Cemetery," would help open up a line of communication with family members about the impact of the project. Specifically, he asked for Howard's "assistance in deciding on the relocation of the gravesites," pledging his "intent to deal with this matter in the most respectful and dignified way possible."[26]

Williams's letter seemed to make it clear that leaving the graves where they were and preserving the site was not an option. The starting point for any negotiation about what would happen to the people buried at Guinea Road and Little River Turnpike was that the roads were going to be widened.

Howard wrote back to Williams immediately, saying he was "very much interested" in the effort and its impact on the cemetery. "I would respectfully suggest that we plan a meeting and/or forum about a month down the road in Fairfax County, Virginia to explain your project, its impact, and public versus private rights in this situation according to eminent domain and other relevant laws. I would very much like to attend." He made it clear from the beginning that his expectation was that he, as a representative of the family, intended to be more than an interested party in the construction project. He was going to be a partner.[27]

On March 27, 2004, Howard sent a letter to a list of Gibson-Parker family members he had compiled in organizing previous family reunions. The cemetery, which he believed contained the remains of some of their ancestors, he wrote, "is threatened with destruction and asphalt. . . . I am respectfully suggesting that we have a responsibility to organize, establish a decision-making process and assure that the remnants of our ancestors and pioneers in Virginia and United States history are treated with dignity, respect and honor."[28]

In early April, Howard wrote to Conley with a series of questions, many of which were outside a reference librarian's purview. These included, "Do you know of a good lawyer who could give a consultation or take this case for the family?" "Does the state of Virginia respect the rights of the dead?" and "Can we handle this matter in a respectful and dignified manner?"

"Let me hear from you, please," Howard pleaded.[29]

Conley may not have set out to be the leading expert on the cemetery at Guinea Road, but whether he liked it or not, that was the position he was in. And he was about to find out that its metaphorical location was in the middle of a firestorm.

Upended

On May 10, 2004, Kerri Barile, the preservation coordinator for the Northern Virginia District of the Virginia Department of Transportation, emailed Conley, saying she had a "bizarre question." She was researching the cemetery in connection with the road project and wondered, "Where did the original information on the whereabouts and details of this cemetery come from? I have looked at all the property deeds and several old maps, and couldn't find any reference to the cemetery."[30]

Conley wrote back a week later. The first time the cemetery was brought to his attention was on a 1980 tax map, he said. He wasn't sure who had first identified it as the Gibson-Parker cemetery, but a file he had inherited in connection with the cemetery index project in 1987 gave it that designation. And in 1994, Badil-Abish had told him that he had access to a family ledger that indicated there were six family burials on Horace Gibson's property. Conley himself had not seen the ledger.[31]

Nevertheless, there were many reasons why the consensus of professional opinion was that there was a cemetery at Little River Turnpike and Guinea Road. The question was how many people were buried there, who they were, and what to do about their remains when the bulldozers rolled in to start the road project.

But the consensus was about to be upended. On May 27, Barile sent a lengthy letter to officials at the Virginia Department of Historic Resources on her work. It concluded, "There is no archival, historical, or physical evidence to suggest that a cemetery is located at the intersection of Little River Turnpike and Guinea Road. VDOT recommends that the presence of a cemetery is derived from oral family tradition, and there are likely no interments in the area."[32]

Barile's report relied heavily on Kay McCarron's study, which was given greater weight than Brian Conley's or Doug Owsley's inspections and reports of multiple graves and fieldstones. In the absence of archival proof, family oral tradition and local lore were all there was to rely on in terms of documentation. And that was deemed insufficient.

When Dennis Howard read the report, he was livid. Once again, he took his concerns straight to the top. In a letter to then Virginia governor Mark Warner, who had succeeded Gilmore, Howard denounced Barile's work as "a down and dirty, exclusive, and unfair shortcut process that may be designed to railroad the Gibson/Parker family and save time and money for the state." Her report, he said, "does not appear to be worth the paper that it's written on."

"Much of world history has been recorded and remembered through oral history," Howard wrote. "Oral history is not wrong because it is oral and written history is not right because it is written. The question is what is the truth? What really happened? Are we rushing to judgment?" He asked for two weeks to go through the process of transitioning off of active-duty service before "the state sends the heavy equipment to dig up and cement family graves." Howard again requested a meeting with state officials to discuss the project as a representative of the family. And he sent a copy of his letter to the *Washington Post*.[33]

Howard was savvy about strategies for keeping the pressure on VDOT, county officials, and even Brian Conley. And he was relentless.

Owsley and Malcolm Richardson were as dismayed as Howard with Barile's letter, though they used more measured language in critiquing it. Their response came in a June 16 letter to Kathleen Kirkpatrick of the Department of Historic Resources, to whom Barile had sent her report. Owsley and Richardson wished, they wrote, to "correct several errors and misstatements" in Barile's work.

Her letter, they said, had stated that McCarron had "completely excavated the entire area to subsoil" and that later archaeological fieldwork also had stripped the accumulated soil on the site. These statements, they wrote, were incorrect. McCarron's survey only removed the topsoil in a small area around an embedded stone. Later explorations also did not attempt to strip the entire area of the purported cemetery.

McCarron and Barile also placed a lot of emphasis on the fact that research establishing a chain of title to the property on which the cemetery was located had shown that the Gibson and Parker families never owned the land. "It is possible, however, that one of the families in the chain of owners of that property did start a cemetery and, after it was established, allowed members of the Parker and Gibson families to be interred there," Owsley and Richardson wrote. They also hinted at another possibility: that there was indeed a cemetery at the location, but it did not include direct descendants of Horace Gibson and Moses Parker. Left unstated was the possibility that Gibson and Parker had ancestors buried at Guinea Road.

Barile and McCarron, Owsley and Richardson pointed out, had emphasized historical property descriptions that mentioned fieldstones planted on Guinea Road and Little River Turnpike as boundary markers. But it appeared, they said, that the two "did not consider that drastic modifications have been made to both Little River Turnpike and Guinea Road after the advent of state-maintained roads beginning in the late 1920s." The original turnpike was probably located where the westbound lanes of the current road were, they wrote, which was some distance from the boundary line of the property in question. Likewise, the eastern Guinea Road boundary had likely shifted.

"There can be no doubt," Owsley and Richardson wrote, "that stone markers depicted in old deeds for the northern and eastern property lines have been long lost during the widening of Little River Turnpike into a divided, four-lane highway and Guinea Road from a single-lane, unpaved track to its current configuration, including a sidewalk."

Similarly, McCarron and Barile noted the absence of deeds referring to a cemetery in the area. This, Owsley and Richardson said, should not have been surprising. It was not necessarily a common practice to describe the location of cemeteries on deeds. It may well have been the case that the cemetery wasn't included because then the land would have been considered suitable only for future burials, which would lower property values. "The practice of not recording cemeteries on deeds is a primary factor in the ongoing destruction of abandoned cemeteries during development in Virginia," they wrote.[34]

Barile noted in her report that McCarron "found that the first mention of a cemetery or burial plot at this corner did not appear until the early 1980s, when a gravesite notation was made on a tax map. . . . No earlier tax maps, county road maps, deed plats, or area atlas maps have any indication of a cemetery at the site."

What McCarron, Barile, Owsley, Richardson, Conley, and everyone else didn't know, though, was that this was not true.

There were references to a cemetery at the intersection both in maps and in historical records. They just hadn't been found yet.

Maps and Deeds

At this point, several pieces of critical information were known about the Little River Turnpike–Guinea Road intersection. They included:

The land on which the cemetery was said to be located was once part of a massive plantation fueled by the labor of enslaved people. Several families in the immediate vicinity were enslavers.

The Gibson and Parker families had founded Ilda and were major landowners in and around it.

Horace Gibson did not own the land on which the cemetery was located. His property in the immediate vicinity was in two locations: across the turnpike to the north and farther down Guinea Road to the south.

Oral tradition (and possibly written records) indicated that Gibson-Parker family members were interred at the site.

African American history had only relatively recently begun to be taken seriously by county officials, and Black historical sites were underrepresented among protected areas.

There had long been talk among local residents that the site contained a cemetery.

Gibson was among those who petitioned for the creation of Jermantown Cemetery in 1878 and was buried there.

Both Little River Turnpike and Guinea Road had been widened multiple times over the years.

Despite numerous efforts to develop the part of the lot where the cemetery was allegedly located, involving houses, grocery stores, gas stations, childcare centers and a Salvation

Army headquarters, nothing had ever been built on the site of the cemetery.

This left a lot of questions, such as: Why was there an oral tradition not just among family members but local residents of the existence of a cemetery if none was there? Why had multiple attempts to develop the site failed? Why was it excluded from the Lee Forest development? The focus was on the question of why there were apparently no references to a cemetery at the intersection in the historical record. For McCarron and Barile, this was nearly dispositive, especially because experts differed as to what the physical evidence found at the site indicated.

It's not unusual for archaeologists to reach conflicting or erroneous conclusions, especially about a site in the middle of a highly developed suburban area that had been overgrown and cleared and overgrown again in cycles through the years. While the scientists argued over the physical evidence at the Guinea Road site, archival researchers and historians set to work on the puzzle of the paper trail. The task would take several years, require additional hands and heads, and lead to many dead ends.

Ultimately, though, they determined that the story started in 1807. That was the year that Richard, Nicholas, and Giles Fitzhugh were ordered to allow a road to be cut through their land to extend Guinea Road to connect with Little River Turnpike.[35] Two years later, a surveyor was appointed to inspect the area "along the new road to the Little River Turnpike near the log meeting house."[36] That changes the picture dramatically. Now the record indicated the presence of a house of worship at the intersection in the early 1800s. And where people worshiped, they often buried their dead.

What about deeds? It turned out one did reference a cemetery. In 1851, the deed that transferred the property from William H. Gooding to Peter Gooding described the boundaries this way: "Beginning on the south side of the Little River Turnpike road below the old grave yard & immediately opposite the lower corner of the said Peter Gooding's land, thence a straight line to a point where the line of the said tract of land crosses the Guinea road."[37]

Other records indicated that a church had once stood at the site. In 1852, when Fairfax County was divided into election districts, the boundary of District No. 4 was described as "up the Falls Church Road to Chichester gate, thence with Chichester Mill road to the old church yard on the Little River Turnpike above Wm Goodings."[38] That is the approximate location of the Little River Turnpike–Guinea Road intersection.

Another reference would turn up in an 1870 record, when the county was divided into townships. The boundary of Lee Township included this description: "thence with the north side of Braddocks road to the Guinea road near Williams old place, thence with the east or lower side of said road to the Little River Turnpike at the old church yard."

In 1930, there is another reference, in a *Fairfax Herald* description of the county's school district boundaries, which matched the township (and later, magisterial district) boundaries. Providence District was described as "beginning at the old 'church yard' (now Gibson's shop) on the Little River Turnpike road." Its last section was described as following "the Guinea road, near Williams' old place; thence with the southeast or lower side of said road, to the 'old church yard,' on the Little River Turnpike road, at Gibson's shop."[39]

So there were indeed references in historical records to both a church and a graveyard at the intersection. How about maps? McCarron and Barile had based a lot of their belief that there was no cemetery on the apparent fact no map had shown one before the 1980s. All subsequent references and investigations seemed to stem from that map.

But it turned out there was in fact an earlier reference. In 1957, as the post–World War II suburban development boom had launched a series of new subdivisions such as Lee Forest, the Virginia Department of Transportation embarked on an effort to widen Little River Turnpike near Guinea Road. Its surveyors produced a map that stands in stark contrast to the hand-drawn plats of bygone days. Gone are the references to things like "Williams old place." Landowners' names are indicated but meticulously referenced by latitude and longitude. The map is nearly covered with technical terms like "Drop R/E," "Comb. Underdrain," and "36.15″ Pipe Req'd."

But there, in tiny letters labeling a small, rectangular plot of land at the southwest corner of Guinea Road and Little River Turnpike, is a notation in plain English of the kind that could have appeared on the faded historic maps: "Old Grave Yard."[40]

The cemetery had not suddenly appeared on a 1980 tax map. And even if county tax officials weren't aware of the 1957 VDOT map at the time they issued the 1980 map, there was a strong reason to include the cemetery on the map: The preponderance of evidence showed it existed.

It's easy to dismiss talk among residents of the existence of a graveyard as mere rumor and hearsay, just as it's easy to dismiss family oral tradition when it comes to researching history. The simple reason that it became commonly accepted by residents that there was a cemetery on the corner of Little River Turnpike and Guinea Road is *that there was a cemetery there.* Many people knew it. Some had seen evidence of it for themselves, both local residents and experienced cemetery experts and archaeologists. That's why the parcel was not included in the 1951 Lee Forest deed, and why every attempt to change the zoning regulations over decades had failed. Public officials weren't spooked by an urban legend that there was a cemetery on the property. After all, rumored cemeteries had been paved over and built upon for decades in Fairfax County and elsewhere. They were concerned because, while the secrets of who was buried at the cemetery remained hidden, evidence of it was there, in plain sight.

Still, the response from would-be developers and certain government officials to those who insisted the cemetery existed was, Prove it. In their June 2004 letter, Owsley and Richardson recommended taking them up on that challenge. "We suggest that methods be used to definitively prove or disprove the existence of a cemetery at the location cited," they wrote. "The best method would be the one purported to have already been performed: to remove the soil in the disturbed zone down to the undisturbed strata."

Proof

With Howard having contacted the governor and the media, and Owsley and Richardson on record disputing McCarron's and Barile's conclusions, VDOT was in a tough position. The conclusion that there was no cemetery was tenuous. There was only one path forward.

They needed to do some real digging. But not to widen the road. At least not yet.

On August 17, 2004, Gary Farrell, a land acquisition specialist with the Virginia Department of Transportation, wrote to Dennis Howard: "This letter is to provide you notice that investigative fieldwork is currently scheduled for the [Gibson/Parker family] cemetery to determine the existence and location of ancestral graves within the area affected by our project. The fieldwork is currently scheduled for September 8th and 9th."

"If gravesites are located during our investigation," Farrell added, "the legal process will then begin through the court process for exhumation and reinterment of the remains."[41]

The Guinea Road Cemetery excavation shortly after it started.
(Courtesy of the Virginia Department of Transportation)

VDOT employee Dave Mitchler, then forty-seven, had been working in construction since he was sixteen. He knew his way around a backhoe. But his experience was largely in the brute force work of moving large amounts of dirt as quickly and efficiently as possible. He hadn't done anything like the task he was now assigned: to gently remove layers of topsoil from the corner lot at Little River Turnpike and Guinea Road to find out what, if anything, lay beneath. Mitchler was big and burly, but he approached the job with a delicate touch, if such a thing is possible with a piece of heavy equipment like a backhoe.[42]

By then, the site was again overgrown. In early September, Mitchler set to work, first removing trees and underbrush from the area where evidence of graves had been found. Then he carefully maneuvered his backhoe and began scraping the surface of the exposed ground until one to two feet of the soil underneath was exposed.

VDOT had contracted with archaeological experts at the Louis Berger Group, Inc., to oversee the dig and assess whether or not there was evidence of burials. When Mitchler had completed his digging work, a team of Berger archaeologists came forward with small trowels and began painstakingly scraping the surface. It didn't take long for them to find what they were looking for: a handful of graves.[43]

Just like that, the mystery was solved, and everything changed. All of the doubts about the existence of a cemetery, all of the challenges to those who had personally uncovered evidence of its presence, and all of the dismissals of family oral tradition and local lore as unverifiable hearsay vanished. But a host of new issues emerged as a result: How many graves were there? What would be done with human remains found at the site? And who exactly was buried there?

The archaeologists and researchers were excited about what else they might find when the area was fully excavated and when the human remains, the remnants of coffins that had contained them, and any artifacts found had been fully analyzed. Dennis Howard, on the other hand, was nervous. All that he had experienced as a Black man growing up in Fairfax County, the research he had conducted into his family's history, and his recent experiences in trying to represent their interests had led him to a place of mistrust of state and county government officials, no matter what organization they worked for.

Howard decided to personally oversee the excavation. As the fieldwork continued, he showed up to observe what was happening. "Mr. Howard's visits were unannounced and provided him with an opportunity to see the archaeologists working unabated (and often unaware of his presence)," the Berger Group later reported.[44]

Because the two days of initial work at the site had achieved such stunning results, Berger and VDOT made arrangements to come back for a second phase and expand the search to try to determine exactly where the remains were and the approximate dimensions of the cemetery. They scheduled the second phase for October 2004.

On October 18, Berger's archaeologists returned to the site. They carefully shoveled and raked the soil by hand, but the amount of construction debris at the site, such as broken cinder blocks and bricks, made it difficult to find evidence of the grave depressions and footstones that had been previously identified at the site. On October 20, Mitchler returned to what had now become a highly sensitive operation. The Berger archaeologists would later thank him "for his masterful backhoe work and his enthusiastic interest in the project."[45] As he expanded the effort to clear the site northward, he continued to uncover additional fieldstones.

Near quitting time, he pulled out one last tree stump at the site. In the process, he uncovered a large stone. Without giving it much thought, Mitchler added it to a pile he had built throughout the day. He parked the backhoe nearby and headed home. But that night, something about the stone kept nagging at him. It was bigger than the others and had appeared white when he removed it from the reddish-brown soil.

Mitchler made a mental note to himself to take a closer look at the stone the next morning.[46]

7

Preservation

ON THE RAINY MORNING of October 21, 2004, Dave Mitchler was the first to arrive at the Guinea Road–Little River Turnpike excavation site. He got there early because he was still filled with curiosity about the large stone he had uncovered with his backhoe the day before. Mitchler found the mud-covered stone where he had left it among several others, carried it to a clean spot at the edge of the road, and vigorously rubbed it with a rag.

Then he saw it: This wasn't just a fieldstone. It was an inscribed tombstone, and he immediately could make out a name, S. A. Williams, and a date of death, 1851.[1] A carved tombstone could provide important clues not just about one individual, but potentially the group of people buried at the site. It raised the possibility that the cemetery might be of greater historical value than previously believed.

An "exciting thing happened yesterday morning," the Virginia Department of Transportation's Andy Williams wrote in an email to archaeologist Malcolm Richardson on October 22. "They uncovered a tombstone about 2 feet down. . . . Wow!" That wasn't all the new round of digging had revealed. The Berger archaeologists had now identified eleven graves, and were certain there were more to be found. "It is unreal how defined the grave shafts are," enthused Williams.[2]

Five days later, Richardson sent an email to Brian Conley at the Virginia Room. "At last check," he reported, "they had 29 graves, extending from the intersection south."[3] In a matter of weeks, the project had gone from one that had been undertaken with some degree of skepticism to the realization that this was a rare find that could provide a wealth of information about the Ilda area. At this point, the National Historic Preservation Act would come into play, and VDOT and its contractor, the Louis Berger Group, would have to be very careful about how they handled the dig and the analysis of what they found.

Name Game

Because it now seemed clear that there must be more to the historical record of the cemetery than had already been uncovered, the next step was to renew the research effort with more intensity. Berger's Megan Rupnik was assigned to take on that task. Kerri Barile would continue to oversee the project for VDOT.

Rupnik would soon make an important discovery: the 1851 deed from William H. Gooding to Peter Gooding referencing an "old cemetery" at the Guinea Road–Little River Turnpike intersection. Doing so took a lot of historical detective work. William, it turned out, had purchased the land twice, in 1851 and 1860, leading to a convoluted chain of title that had led previous researchers astray.

Conley, too, delved into deed and tax records, and did some initial work on attempting to identify S. A. Williams. On November 6, 2004, he sent a letter to Andy Williams and others updating them on what he had found: "There is little in the way of hard evidence to use in identifying this site, but I believe the available facts point to the cemetery as an ante-bellum community burial ground for the small free Black community in the area. It may even have begun as a slave cemetery for slaves owned by either the Fitzhughs or some unknown tenant. This means that members of the Gibson and Parker families may very well be buried at this site as claimed by [Hareem Badil-Abish], but it is certainly not their exclusive family cemetery. Lacking a better name I will henceforth be referring to this burial ground as the Guinea Road Cemetery."

On November 15, Barile told Conley that based on the evidence at hand, she would likely make the case to the Virginia Department of Historic Resources that the site was eligible for inclusion on the National Register of Historic Places. This would mean that the excavators and investigators would have to take great care in handling artifacts and remains found at the site and would need to negotiate with interested parties about what to do with the latter. "The next step will be to determine if our [road] project will have an adverse effect on this eligible site," she wrote. "Uhhh, I think we know the answer to that one, too!"

At this stage, Dennis Howard was surely happy to be vindicated about the existence of the cemetery. But as the de facto Gibson-Parker family representative, and as someone who had spent decades gathering information about his ancestors, he would remain guarded at every stage of the process.

Toward the end of the year, Howard sent Conley a holiday card with Mickey Mouse in full Santa regalia on the front. "Great job on your research and 11/6/04 letter," he wrote. "We will talk in early 2005, God willing."[4]

On January 5, 2005, Howard let his fingers do the talking, penning a letter to Williams and copying Conley and others. Referencing Conley's November 6 missive, he said the researcher "refers to the site as the Guinea Road Cemetery. Is the state of

Virginia and/or Fairfax County, Virginia attempting to re-write history and write out the contribution of the African American Community?"[5]

Quite the contrary, Conley replied on January 20: "History is 're-written' whenever new facts are discovered. I believe my November 6 letter made it clear that the Guinea Road Cemetery is important not simply as a burial ground for one family, but for an entire African American community." Conley noted that his authority to rename the cemetery extended only to records kept at the library anyway.

"I believe that referencing site 44FX 1664 as the 'Guinea Road Cemetery' more accurately reflects its probable origin as a community graveyard, and recognizes that there could potentially be many more people interested in this site than previously thought," he wrote.[6]

The Berger Group issued its initial report on the archaeological investigation in February 2005. It said VDOT had chosen the location to be explored based on "limited historical documentation," prior archaeological work, and oral history. The project area, the report stated, extended 110 feet north and south within the VDOT right-of-way along the western edge of Guinea Road, starting at its intersection with Little River Turnpike. It went westward between eight and thirty-two feet from the edge of the sidewalk on Guinea. There was no excavation in the residential lot of the house built in 1993, or under Little River Turnpike to the north. The archaeologists found graves right up to the edge of the defined area. That meant it was unlikely they found all the remains that were interred at the site.

"No buffer area clear of grave shafts was identified at the northern end of the project area . . . and therefore there may be additional grave shafts located under the service road to the north of the project area," the Berger report concluded. "Finally, no buffer area clear of grave shafts was located to the west of the project area. There may be additional graves in the residential lot to the west."

Rupnik's archival research for Berger was extensive, involving reviewing files at the Virginia Department of Historic Resources; historical texts and maps at the Library of Virginia in Richmond; the collections of the Fairfax County Public Library; and tax and deed records at the Fairfax County Courthouse. Still, some of the initial conclusions would require further review and updating. For example, the report said that Ilda was believed to have been "a community of freedmen, based on information provided by descendants of its early residents, particularly the Gibson and Parker families, although little written historical information has been located on the community."[7] But it was not the case that the community consisted solely of freed slaves. Berger's final report four years later would correctly note that "the crossroads area where the Gibson and Parker families settled would eventually become the racially mixed community of Ilda."[8]

As the Berger Group was putting the finishing touches on its report, Barile previewed it for Conley and said Berger, too, would reach the conclusion that the cemetery was eligible for inclusion on the National Register of Historic Places. VDOT would then coordinate with the Department of Historic Resources on next steps, leading to a memorandum of agreement on how to proceed. "This will likely involve additional research and probably eventually excavation," she wrote.[9]

In the meantime, Dennis Howard continued to seethe at Conley's name change for the cemetery and the fact that everyone seemed to be buying into the new nomenclature. In a letter to Conley dated February 12, 2005, he addressed him as "My Dear Brother Brian" and wrote that in 1992, Hareem Badil-Abish had introduced Conley to him "as a fine, decent, sensitive man and a wonderful historian who supported his research." But on the issue of the name, Howard wrote, Conley had "missed the mark."

"I do not like the idea of changing the name of the Gibson-Parker Cemetery to the 'Guinea Road Cemetery.' The Horace Gibson and Moses Parker stories are stories that rival the Alex Haley story told in the book *Roots*. This story is an American story, a Virginia story and a Fairfax County story that embraces the American dream and vision of inclusivity, diversity, tolerance, and a level playing field. We can all be proud of this story. This is a story that should be told. . . . Keep the name the same."[10]

Under the Road

Howard also reiterated a question he had raised earlier: Since the excavation team had reported the existence of graves under the sidewalk at Guinea Road, did that mean VDOT had paved remains over in previous road-widening efforts?

In early March, VDOT officials wrote to Howard to address this and other issues he had raised. The archaeologists had discovered, they said, that the cemetery area was covered with one to three feet of road construction debris, probably from a road-widening project in the early 1960s. There had been no road-widening work since then. No human remains had been found in the previous work at the site.

Still, VDOT acknowledged that "it is not known if additional graves are under the road itself. VDOT recognizes the potential for graves to exist under the roadway, and future archaeological work in this area might resolve this uncertainty. We agree that it is our responsibility to explore all potential avenues for inquiry in determining how potential graves under the roadway will be handled. Any decisions regarding this work will include input from several state and local agencies, as well as you and your family."[11]

The VDOT team also invited Howard and other family members to meet with them to discuss the project and the next phase of work. Howard had requested such a meeting on behalf of the family almost a year earlier.

On March 28, 2005, VDOT's Kerri Barile wrote to the Department of Historic Resources with an update on the work at the cemetery site and a request for an expedited review of its historical impact. "This project is time-sensitive and the next phase of work will require extended coordination with multiple parties," she wrote.

In the letter, Barile addressed previous research efforts. She noted concerns about the conclusions drawn from contract archaeologist Kay McCarron's 1990 report on the site. "Within the past few months," Barile wrote, "it has been suggested that the reporting on McCarron's fieldwork is not accurate, and this survey should not be relied upon as a comprehensive examination of the project area." She also noted Doug Owsley and Malcolm Richardson's 1991 survey of the site, saying that "their studies, although informative, were inconclusive."[12]

Owsley was not pleased with that characterization. He wrote that he and Richardson, in the course of their survey, "were able to almost immediately locate, with our feet, a line of field stones beneath a heavy layer of leaf litter. Several shallow depressions were also noted. Using probes, we were able to verify the presence of six burial shafts." Such results, he argued, were hardly inconclusive.[13]

An Agreement

On June 3, 2005, Howard finally got the meeting he had been asking for. The purpose was to hammer out a memorandum of agreement between all interested parties about how to proceed with the excavation and analysis of the graveyard and ultimately the road-widening project. Such a memo was a required part of the process now that a cemetery with significant historical value was verified to exist at the Guinea Road site. In particular, Howard's buy-in was critical. He was the link to the Gibson-Parker descendants, and if they were opposed to any part of the process, it could come to a grinding halt.

The meeting convened at 10:30 a.m. at the headquarters of the Virginia Department of Historic Resources in Richmond. It was not, judging from the minutes, a contentious discussion. Whether Howard was worn down by the process or simply eager to do his part and compromise is hard to tell. But what is clear is that he was willing to work with state, local, and now federal officials (the Federal Highway Administration sent a representative to the meeting, because VDOT anticipated receiving federal assistance for the project) to reach a mutually agreeable solution.[14]

At the meeting, Kerri Barile, Andy Williams, and other officials led a general discussion about what to do with the graves that had already been located at the site and those that might be found in future work. They presented three possible options: removal of all graves, removal of only the graves within the VDOT impact area, or leaving the graves in place. The last option did not appear to get serious consideration. From a political and transportation planning perspective, leaving the remains where they were and not proceeding with the road construction was a nonstarter.

Some Gibson-Parker descendants would later raise questions about why the graves needed to be disturbed. But as Sharon Bulova, who then represented the cemetery area on the Fairfax County Board of Supervisors, later put it in an interview: "You don't have a free right turn lane there. It'll help unkink traffic." Unkinking traffic was an imperative that could not be ignored, even by a public official like Bulova who had a track record of supporting efforts to document and protect the area's historic resources.[15] Even the Department of Historic Resources acknowledged the reality of the situation. "Our mission is to encourage the preservation of historic sites while balancing respect for the dead with the reality of the fact that land use has changed," said its director, Kathleen Kilpatrick, in early 2006.[16]

This is not to suggest that the government officials involved in the meeting and the ongoing process were not respectful and open to considering the family's requests. Once the state had acknowledged the existence of the cemetery, VDOT and other agencies dealt with the process of unearthing remains, and determining what to do with them, with sensitivity.

After VDOT presented its options at the meeting, Howard asked whether the agency would be able to remove the graves and still get its road-widening project done on time. He wondered whether VDOT had the budget for this kind of undertaking. Barile assured him that the agency had the time and the money to complete the work as scheduled.

VDOT, Barile acknowledged, would ultimately have to determine where the boundaries of the cemetery were. Howard asked whether the agency was willing to close the roads to reach a conclusion on that issue. Barile said VDOT would temporarily close Guinea Road and a small access road to Little River Turnpike to probe for graves in these areas. Such work would have to be done in stages, and some of it just before road construction was to begin.

The representative of the Department of Historical Resources said that in general, the agency preferred to leave burials in place unless there was a compelling reason to remove them. But, the meeting minutes note, "she expressed concern . . . with the concept of human remains being buried beneath a transportation facility." In other words, allowing thousands of cars per day to zoom over human bodies in their last resting place made her queasy.

Howard said he would prefer removal of the remains. Everyone agreed.

That raised the question of where to place them. VDOT recommended Pleasant Valley Memorial Park, located about a half mile east of the Guinea Road–Little River Turnpike intersection, on the property where Gooding's Tavern once stood. Representatives of Pleasant Valley had said they would be honored to receive the remains, provided that VDOT pay for a new gravesite and erect a marker noting the history of the Guinea Road Cemetery and who was buried there. Howard was pleased with this arrangement, because several family members already were interred at Pleasant Valley.

Howard still had a couple of other concerns. First, he asked how the results of the excavation and the results of the analysis of the remains would be publicized. Very little had been written about the history of African Americans in Fairfax County, he noted, and he wanted more than a dry consultant's report to address what had been learned about Ilda and the cemetery. VDOT officials said they'd be open to a number of different ways of making information about the site available to the public. These included placing a historical marker at the site, separate from the marker that would be erected at Pleasant Valley Cemetery.

Howard then raised an issue that only he among the people in the room could fully understand and apply to the project under discussion. He brought up the Pines. It was all too fresh in Gibson-Parker family members' minds how in that case government officials had swooped in, taken their land, and utterly disrupted their lives—all in the name of a school construction project that never actually took place.

Howard asked a simple, direct question: All of the plans, all of the pledges to the family that money would be spent to respectfully dig up, transfer, and rebury the remains of their ancestors—was this really going to happen? Or would it be added to the list of broken promises made to African Americans in the county?

VDOT officials assured him that they would do as they pledged. In fact, they said, they thought the transfer of the remains could be completed in time to coincide with a Gibson-Parker family reunion tentatively scheduled for the fall of 2006.

All that remained now was the paperwork: a formal memorandum of agreement and, in all likelihood, a court order mandating that the work be completed as laid out in the memo. After the embarrassment of mistaken archaeological analyses, the hue and cry among family members and neighbors about the potential disturbance of a cemetery, and the ongoing pressure to ease traffic backups at the intersection, everyone was going to play this one by the book.

That was doubly true because word of the situation at the cemetery was going public, and not just among neighbors and commuters who had noticed the signs of excavation on Guinea Road. In July 2005, *Preservation,* the magazine of the National Trust for Historic Preservation, published an article on the site headlined "Paving over the Dead." The burials at this "nondescript suburban corner" that "bears little resemblance to an historic site" were threatened, the story stated. It also noted that Dennis Howard had "aggressively lobbied" Virginia officials to bury any remains found at another location.[17]

Operating with the appropriate level of care meant the gears of bureaucracy would grind away for a time. It would take another eight months for the memorandum of agreement to be negotiated, drafted, lawyered, and drafted some more. The final version was issued in February 2006. After several "Whereas" clauses, "pursuant to" stipulations, and one big "Now Therefore," VDOT was given the authority to develop a plan for the excavation, removal, analysis, and reinterment of human remains at the Guinea Road Cemetery. They would do so "in consultation" with the Virginia state historic preservation officer and Dennis Howard. VDOT agreed, in addition to placing a historical marker at the site, to "implement one additional concept," such as a website or small museum exhibit, to publicize the findings of the excavation and research into the remains. But they couldn't spend more than ten thousand dollars on it.[18]

On February 24, 2006, Fairfax County Circuit Court Judge Jane Marum Roush—in a courthouse just steps away from the historic building in which Horace Gibson had won legal battles against a horse thief and a violent, harassing neighbor—declared it was "adjudged, ordered and decreed" that the project proceed according to the stipulations laid out in the memorandum of agreement.[19]

What followed next was more digging, both literally and in archives, libraries, and public records offices. The Guinea Road Cemetery had more to reveal.

Excavation and Examination

With all of the paperwork in place, the Louis Berger team returned to the site on March 20, 2006. They first turned to the twenty-nine previously identified interments and found that, when they were fully excavated, they actually represented eighteen burials. The other presumed graves proved to be soil anomalies or postholes for utility poles that had been moved when the road was previously widened.[20]

Then, in early April, the archaeologists turned to the northern portion of the site, which hadn't been examined previously. There they found an additional ten graves. They kept working northward until they reached an area free of graves that was wider than the distance between any row of burials within the cemetery. This they determined to be the northern edge of the cemetery. The Berger team also excavated part of the residential lot for the first time. They found no grave shafts there and declared it to be the western boundary of the cemetery.

From April 10 to April 19, the archaeologists excavated the grave shafts. In one of them, they found a small fragment of a smooth, marked gravestone with a portion of a letter engraved on it, resembling in style the large S. A. Williams stone. They also uncovered a total of thirty-six rectangular stones that may have been grave markers. Half of the stones were granite and showed evidence of having been cut. The rest were irregularly shaped and showed no sign of cutting. The Berger team also uncovered and cataloged 3,348 artifacts from the graves—mostly machine-cut nails but also coffin hardware, wood samples, buttons, snaps, woven cloth, yarn, and bottle glass.

The presence of cut nails meant that the burials must have come sometime after 1830, when such nails came into use (as opposed to hand-forged nails). Buttons made from china and pressed glass could only have been made after 1840. Coffin hardware, particularly hinges, were dated to sometime after 1861.

Then there were the human remains. A total of thirty-five individuals were ultimately found: eighteen adults, sixteen children, and one whose age couldn't be determined. All of the burials were oriented east to west, and all of the coffins were hexagonal.

According to the Berger report, modern utility construction hadn't disturbed the graves as much as the growth of tree roots had. For example, a quarter of the coffin outline in one grave had been destroyed by the construction of a fiber optic cable line, but no human remains were located there. A gas pipeline trench had gone through another shaft but had not disturbed the coffin.

"In deference to the family," Berger later reported, "screening was used to shield the excavation of human remains from the public. . . . All human remains were treated in a respectful and dignified manner. No burials were left exposed after work hours or over a weekend. All excavated remains were transported to a secure location provided by the VDOT." Dennis Howard, the

Berger report said, complimented Berger senior archaeologist Charles Rinehart on several occasions on the professionalism and respect of the workers.[21] "No one ate, smoked or listened to the radio as each bone was removed, wrapped in foil and identified," VDOT reported.[22] But neighbors said they could look into the excavated areas during the day and see the small colored flags marking remains and artifacts the archaeologists had located. They were allowed to inspect the S. A. Williams stone after it was found.[23]

When it came time to analyze the remains, they were sent to Radford University, about thirty-five miles southwest of Richmond, where Donna and Cliff Boyd, a husband-and-wife team of anthropologists, intensively examined them. In ten of the burials, no bones or teeth were preserved at all. Bone preservation in the remaining burials was fair to poor, making it difficult to draw definitive conclusions about them. As a result, the race of the individuals studied could only be determined in the case of six sets of remains. All were African American.

Nine of the buried skeletons showed evidence of arthritis. One elderly woman had traces of muscular stress on her upper legs. An old man had bone stress from the muscles of his arms and legs. The collarbones of two men showed signs of stress. And one man, middle-aged when he died, had a "robust right arm," another indication of stress. The teeth of all of those identified were in "extraordinarily bad shape," the Berger report said. One woman had twenty-six cavities.

Taken together, "it is likely that these . . . represent skeletal manifestations of the functional stresses of slavery for African Americans in the 19th century," the Boyds concluded. The Berger team reported that "at least some and perhaps all of these burials are Blacks who were probably enslaved for all or most of their lives"—while including the caveat that "it would be easy to exaggerate the significance of these indices."

Preservation
———

Archival Analysis

All of this scientific analysis shed a fascinating light on what was underground at the Guinea Road Cemetery. But who, exactly, were these people—especially the mysterious S. A. Williams? Trying to determine that would require more research.

That's when Maddy McCoy, a freshly minted historic preservation intern at the Fairfax City Regional Library, entered the picture. In the summer of 2005, she began looking anew at the history of the Ilda area and the families who lived there. She undertook the task with relish, and it would be life-changing for her.

McCoy is the type of person who is equally at home hacking her way through the underbrush of an abandoned graveyard or the dusty archives of a records office. Tell her you're interested in Ilda and the Guinea Road Cemetery, and she'll immediately begin explaining chains of title to properties, the significance of road orders, and the gold mine that is the Fairfax County Circuit Court Historic Records Office. Asked if she has any documents related to the Guinea Road project, she arrives with box after overstuffed box of memos, email printouts, and dozens and dozens of pages of handwritten notes from interviews, property research, and genealogical investigations.

Plowing through all of it is like experiencing a police procedural TV show from the inside. Pages are filled with notes taken from historic documents, texts, and newspaper clippings. The margins are littered with question marks and exclamation points, along with sometimes cryptic notes from interviews and field surveys. The material, on the whole, looks like it would be best displayed on a wall-sized piece of corkboard, connected with lengths of yarn. McCoy's belief in the ability of data and documents to reveal untold stories from unheard voices in the past is near-religious. At the same time, she's fully comfortable discussing whether or not mystical forces may have been at work on Guinea Road to protect the cemetery, referencing African symbology.

After her work on the Guinea Road project, McCoy would go on to develop the Slavery Inventory Database, an exhaustive catalogue of records on the lives of the enslaved. She then founded a public history consultancy that has, among other projects, worked with the Virginia Theological Seminary in Alexandria on a reparations project relating to people enslaved at the institution. McCoy, who was adopted as a child, remembers meeting Dennis Howard for the first time in the Virginia Room. "We had the exact same experience in school" of facing a near-impossible task of tracing their families' histories, she said. "It was a moment of extreme clarity."[24]

As the archaeological work continued, McCoy, her supervisor Brian Conley, and Berger's Megan Rupnik delved into their research, hoping to shed as much light as possible on exactly what transpired at Guinea Road and Little River Turnpike over the centuries. Their work would result in a much clearer timeline of events and hypotheses about who might have been buried at Guinea Road. But some questions would remain unanswered.

In the meantime, Howard went ahead with planning for a family reunion in the fall of 2006. The excavation and analysis of the remains at the site appeared to be on schedule to allow for reinterment of remains at Pleasant Valley cemetery during the reunion.

"Dear Family and Friends," he wrote in a letter dated March 3, 2006. "The Commonwealth of Virginia, the Fairfax County Government and the Gibson-Parker family will celebrate the Ilda Community of Fairfax, Virginia, the weekend of September 30, 2006–October 1, 2006." He enclosed a draft program for the weekend and a copy of the court order on transfer of the remains, saying, "we are very pleased with the results."

As preparations for the reunion and the reinterment of remains continued, Conley and McCoy made an awkward discovery: of the six Gibson-Parker children said to be buried at Guinea Road according to family records (three of Horace and Margaret Gibson and three of Page and Matilda Parker), it was very likely that at least three, and maybe four, were buried elsewhere. Several Gibson children were interred at Jermantown Cemetery—a logical choice, given Horace Gibson's role in establishing the cemetery. A number of the Parker children were buried at the Second Baptist Church of Falls Church, where the family had worshiped before the First Baptist Church of Merrifield was created.

Based on the physical and documentary evidence, Conley told Howard in May, "it is my belief that none of the [Badil-Abish]-referenced Parker/Gibson ancestors are buried in the Guinea Road Cemetery."[25]

This threw Howard for a loop, especially since it came while he was in the midst of planning a family reunion whose centerpiece would be the reinterment of what he believed to be his ancestors' remains at Pleasant Valley. "It is early in the day with this research," he wrote to Conley on June 6. "The sun is high in the sky. Why does a historian-archivist have to guess at this point and say what is likely or could be? Don't we owe the public and history the truth here? Why rush?"

Howard noted that Conley had focused on the names that Badil-Abish had provided but that there were several other Gibson-Parker children who might be buried at the cemetery on Guinea Road. He also pointed out that the Virginia Department of Transportation had yet to establish the eastern boundary of the cemetery, meaning that more bodies could be buried under Guinea Road. "Let's hold this ground until new information and facts cause us to change," he wrote.[26]

The problem was that the Historical Marker Committee of the Fairfax County History Commission was in the process of drafting language to appear on the monument to the Guinea Road Cemetery to be erected at Pleasant Valley when the remains were reinterred. "While there is much about the Guinea Road Cemetery that we do not yet know, we can be certain that the cemetery was in use before the Gibsons and Parkers moved to Fairfax," Conley wrote in comments on the proposed text for the marker. "I would not cast the Gibson/Parker names in iron until we can confirm the burials on this site."[27]

The resulting text was a compromise involving this interpretation and Howard's insistence that the marker at least put the cemetery in a broader context. It reads:

Virginia aristocrat William Fitzhugh was granted 21,996 acres in 1694: The Ravensworth tract, which was divided into northern and southern halves in 1701 and subsequently subdivided among Fitzhugh heirs throughout the 18th and 19th centuries. The cemetery located at Guinea Road and Little River Turnpike (Route 236) was part of the northern half of the original tract. The community of Ilda grew around this cemetery in the late 19th century. Families of local tenant farmers, African American slaves and Freedmen are believed to have been buried at the Guinea Road Cemetery. The remains were reinterred at this site by the Virginia Department of Transportation in 2006.

Now, 140 years after Horace Gibson and Moses Parker moved to Fairfax County, eighteen years after Brian Conley first catalogued the Guinea Road Cemetery, and two years after the process of excavating and analyzing the site—at a cost of more than $300,000—was completed, the existence of the people buried at Guinea Road was officially affirmed, and they were to receive a dignified burial.

"Well, it's on," Howard wrote in an update to family members on plans for the reunion. "See you there."

Moving Day

The morning of Saturday, September 30, 2006, dawned bright and clear in Northern Virginia. Temperatures would rise into the high 60s, perfect weather for a family reunion and a solemn outdoor celebration.[28]

Dennis Howard woke with a song in his head: "You've Got to Move," an African American spiritual. "To me, God got ready for these people to get out from underneath the ground," he said. "God got tired of the manner in which they were being treated."[29]

More than one hundred Gibson-Parker family members had descended on the area that was once Ilda, from as far away as Norfolk, Virginia, and southern New Jersey. At 11:00 a.m., they gathered at the First Baptist Church of Merrifield. In the gleaming white building that had been the center of the family's life for generations, they prayed, sang hymns, and listened to a sermon on Psalm 118:22: "The stone which the builders refused has become the headstone of the corner."[30]

Then came an event that would have astonished the founding families of Ilda: Fairfax County police led a procession of family members' cars to Pleasant Valley Memorial Park. They followed roughly the same route that Ilda's African American children did on their daily trek home from the Black school in Merrifield.

At the cemetery, the family members were met by dignitaries representing the county government, the Virginia Department of Transportation, and various other institutions. After a Fairfax Police honor guard solemnly opened the ceremony, there were more hymns, prayers, and speeches. The Fairfax County Board of Supervisors issued a proclamation congratulating the Gibson-Parker family on the celebration and expressing "joy and appreciation for the heritage and contributions woven into the fabric of Fairfax County by their forebears." Then Howard unveiled the historical marker. The dead of the Guinea Road Cemetery were quietly laid to rest in their new home, tucked into a secluded spot at Pleasant Valley. A small roadway curves nearby, but there's almost no traffic on it, and there are no burials underneath.

The day's events ended with an informational presentation at the cultural center of Northern Virginia Community College, across the road from Pleasant Valley and less than a mile east of the Ilda crossroads. The three-hour program began with an opening prayer, remarks by a local minister, and musical selections. Then Charles Rinehart, the Berger team's chief archaeologist, took the stage. In an hour-long presentation, followed by a fifteen-minute question-and-answer session, he described the meticulous efforts of Berger and VDOT personnel at the site. Every one of the people whose remains they were able to exhume and analyze, he said, "definitely led a hard life of labor, consistent with slaves and former slaves."

Among the photos displayed was one showing an excavated grave. Some of the more than one hundred family members in attendance audibly gasped. What was to the investigators, researchers, and archaeologists a scientific, historical, and cultural revelation, was to family members something real and visceral. What they saw was visual evidence of the remains of their living, breathing ancestors, whose life in bondage was so difficult that evidence of the sheer physical toll it took on their bodies was identifiable more than one hundred years after they had been laid to rest.

Maddy McCoy was in the audience for the presentation and answered some of the questions from family members about the history of Ilda and the family. She was in the process of writing up her "voluminous research" on the Guinea Road area, Brian Conley said.[31]

As the day's events ended at around 10:00 p.m., Howard had reached the culmination of a decades-long quest. His thoughts took him back to the family tree assignment from Mrs. Bouilly at

Stratford Junior High. "It took me 40 years to complete, but I did complete it," he said. "I never forgot the challenge."[32]

Months earlier, a *Washington Post* columnist had asked Howard what he would tell his ancestors if he could speak to them. He said, "I would let them know that I held the fort and did the best I could in terms of preserving their memories and contributions."[33]

Finish Line

After the reunion and reinterment ceremony, VDOT's Andy Williams sent a congratulatory message to various people who worked on the project. "It has been a long drawn-out process and has garnered a lot of attention, but the end result is that the descendants and the community are satisfied and Fairfax County's history is richer because of it," he wrote. "It is good to see everyone smiling as we cross the finish line!"[34]

The finish line of the archaeological investigation was the starting line for the actual widening of Guinea Road. That effort didn't get underway until 2007, and it soon became apparent that not everybody had smiling faces about the project. In June, there were a series of attacks on VDOT equipment and property near the Guinea Road site. One of the incidents involved a fire set in a construction company storage area, which was also tagged with graffiti warning that the "wrath of God" would come to the project. In another, someone fired a pellet gun at the windshield of a piece of construction equipment, shattering it. Capitol Paving employee Ray Khattab, who was working on the project, reported that he and his neighbors had received an unsigned letter in their mailboxes criticizing the construction project and overdevelopment in general.

"Someone is very upset with the disturbance of that cemetery," Khattab said.[35]

Around the same time, fliers began to appear in the neighborhood headlined, "Save the Guinea Road Graveyard." They noted the presence of a cemetery at the crossroads and said VDOT "intends to dig up this graveyard to widen the intersection." The flier pointed out that dozens of skeletons had already been removed and relocated, and said VDOT had plans to dig up more soon.

"The descendants of the people buried in this graveyard were *not* given a choice in the matter of the graves being dug up. (VDOT would like you to think that the descendants are happy with the decision, but in reality several of the descendants are upset about it.) . . . It's time to send a message to VDOT, our county government, and our state government, and let them know that we are fed up with the moving of graves just because someone wants to widen the road or build on the site."[36]

The message went unheeded. The road project proceeded as planned.

In December 2007 and January 2008, the Louis Berger team returned to the Guinea Road site to excavate an area underneath the sidewalk on the west side of the road that couldn't be disturbed until the construction was partially completed. They found two more grave shafts with sets of remains. At that point, they concluded that they had determined the size and dimensions of the cemetery: a little less than 3,000 square feet, or about three-quarters of an acre.

Berger's final report on the project runs to well over three hundred pages. It includes a detailed summary of the cemetery's historical context, along with ethnobotanical analysis, information on soil stratigraphy, osteological studies, and more. The age of coffin hardware and garment buttons, researchers concluded, suggested that the cemetery was in use from circa 1850 to 1875.

"The archaeological data recovery has exhausted the site's research potential," the report concluded.[37]

In June 2008, Howard wrote a memo to Mary Lipsey, who was heading up an effort launched by Sharon Bulova to document the history of Fairfax County's Braddock District. That included the Guinea Road Cemetery. In the memo, he noted VDOT's initial report "denying any graves at this site, notwithstanding family oral tradition" and pointed out that it wasn't until a "family representative wrote to former Governor Mark Warner asking for verification that no graves existed at site" that the excavation had taken place.[38]

Howard clearly hadn't forgotten the difficulty of the process, but apparently bygones were bygones by September 19, 2008. That's when he, other family members, and various local county and state officials gathered again at Pleasant Valley cemetery to rebury the remains found in the two grave shafts identified in the Berger excavation in late 2007 and early 2008.

In another solemn ceremony involving prayers, songs, and politicians' speeches, the remains were placed in the ground. There they joined their fellow residents of the Ilda area—enslaved people who worked the land before the community was founded, and also possibly freed people and local tenant farmers.

On November 23, 2010, John P. Cooke, by then the VDOT archaeologist, sent one last letter to the Virginia Department of Historic Resources. It detailed the actions taken to meet the requirements of the 2006 memorandum of agreement. These included issuing and distributing final reports on the archaeological investigation, erecting the historical marker, and producing an educational poster and brochure for display at the Fairfax County Library.

"This completes the stipulations detailed in the MOA for which VDOT was responsible," Cooke wrote. The long saga of the Guinea Road Cemetery was over.[39]

8

Redemption

ON A BITTERLY COLD afternoon in mid-December 2010, a small group of people gathered at the Little River Turnpike–Guinea Road intersection to take care of one last piece of unfinished business: the dedication of an Ilda historical marker. The temperature wouldn't rise out of the 30s that day, but a Fairfax County Fire and Rescue honor guard was undaunted, marching confidently over the snow- and ice-covered ground to the place where the covered marker stood.[1]

The group, including Dennis Howard, various Gibson-Parker family members, and several community leaders, had already enjoyed an informational program in the warmth of the Jewish Community Center of Northern Virginia across the street.[2] So they kept the pomp and ceremony to a minimum. With the sun low in the sky, they held a candlelit ceremony and unveiled the marker, which reads:

Ilda, a community located at the intersection of Guinea Road and Little River Turnpike, came into existence after the Civil War and lasted into the first half of the twentieth century. It originated when two freedmen, Horace Gibson and Moses Parker, purchased property from the Gooding family on the north side of the turnpike and established a blacksmith shop. In time, a racially mixed community grew to include a post office. According to tradition, the name "Ilda" was a contraction of the name Matilda Gibson Parker. Descendants of Gibson and Parker were probably buried in a nearby cemetery, perhaps originally created to accommodate Gooding family slaves. The remains were relocated in 2008.

And with that, everyone went on their way, and Ilda's story took up permanent residence on Little River Turnpike, not far from where Andy Williams of the Virginia Department of Transportation had posted his huge metal sign, hoping to draw out anyone with knowledge of the cemetery. The irony was that with the new right-turn lane on Guinea Road, VDOT had at least temporarily fixed the problem of traffic backing up in the right-hand

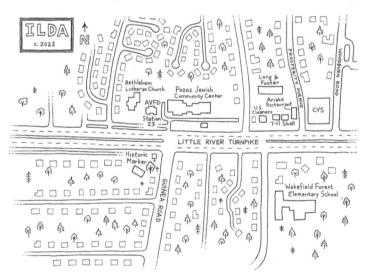

Map by Gregory Nemec

lane of Little River Turnpike, so most drivers would now zoom past the marker without being able to read what it says.

Epistemological Challenge

There was, of course, more to Ilda's story than the marker could contain. And some questions about the nearby cemetery remain unanswered.

"The Guinea Road Cemetery presents us with a very unusual epistemological challenge," the Louis Berger team said in its final report on its investigation into the graveyard.[3] The historical documentary evidence for the existence of a cemetery was thin, yet there it was, buried underneath 150 years of accumulated road and construction debris. Gibson-Parker family members were convinced, based on oral tradition, of the graveyard's location. They were right. But it turned out to be bigger and more historically significant than they imagined.

Since Maddy McCoy and others uncovered multiple references to an "old cemetery" and an "old church yard" starting in 1851, along with documentary evidence of a meetinghouse in the early 1800s, it's possible that the cemetery was used by both white and Black residents over several decades. It may have started as a white cemetery associated with the meetinghouse and later come into use by local African Americans. The Berger report didn't entertain this possibility because only the 1851 reference to an old cemetery had been uncovered by the time the report was issued, and Berger's researchers pegged the earliest remains as dating from about 1850. So they concluded the 1851 reference couldn't have referred to the Guinea Road Cemetery.

What of the mysterious S. A. Williams? The headstone indicated that he or she died in 1851, at the age of eleven. McCoy, Berger's Megan Rupnik, and others combed through historical records to try to come up with a definitive answer to who the child was, and never did. Berger concluded, based on what it called "fairly strong circumstantial evidence," that it most likely was Samuel Williams, a white child. His family lived near the intersection of Guinea Road and Braddock Road, two miles south of Little River Turnpike. He was listed as ten years old on the 1850 census but did not appear on the 1860 census. This explanation, however, raised several questions, such as, what was a white child doing buried at a cemetery in which a number of those interred were African American? Why wouldn't he have been buried at a family cemetery nearer to home? The Berger team could only surmise that the gravestone may have been taken from a disused family graveyard years after the child's burial and dumped at the Guinea Road Cemetery.[4]

Not only was it impossible to determine conclusively the identity of S. A. Williams, it was a challenge to ascertain even generally who the other people buried in the cemetery were. Some, if not all, were clearly African Americans who had been enslaved. The best that the researchers could come up with was that at least some of those buried at Guinea Road likely were among the eighty people enslaved by William, Peter, and William H. Gooding. Others could have been some of the fifty-eight people formerly enslaved by William Fitzhugh, who were granted freedom in his 1850 will.[5] Finally, the idea that Gibson-Parker ancestors were among those whose remains were found was still a possibility, because so many of the remains were poorly preserved.

"We still don't know who was buried at Guinea Road," McCoy wrote months after Berger issued its final report.[6] We still don't have the full answer today.

Hate and Faith

It would be nice to think that the discovery of the Guinea Road Cemetery and the dedication of historical markers recognizing the sacrifices and contributions of African Americans in the area ushered in an era of peaceful coexistence in what had once been known as Ilda. It also wouldn't be entirely true.

On the night of April 10, 2017, the Jewish Community Center of Northern Virginia was again attacked by a white supremacist vandal, who spray-painted "Hitler Was Right," a Nazi SS symbol, and a swastika on its exterior brick walls. The hateful act was made even more painful by the fact that it occurred during the holiday of Passover.[7]

To make matters worse, this time the attacker struck a nearby church as well. Banners in front of the Little River United Church of Christ, about a half mile east of the community center, were also vandalized. A swastika was spray-painted over the church's Holy Week schedule, and a sign reading, "Honor God, Say NO to Anti-Muslim Bigotry," also was painted over. A twenty-year-old local man was arrested and charged with hate-related offenses in connection with the incidents.

The attacks were egregious not just because of the hateful symbolism and the timing but because of each institution's demonstrated commitment to equality and freedom of worship. In 1955, during the throes of segregation, the Little River United Church of Christ was founded as the Congregational Christian Church for the express purpose of providing a place for all races to worship together. "That same call led us in 2001 to become open to and affirming of LGBT folks, including full access to the rites of ordination and marriage," the church's website says. "Today, we build on our heritage of proclaiming God's radically inclusive love to our congregation, neighborhood, and world."[8]

The website also has a section devoted to addressing the fact that the church sits on land once owned by the Gooding family and worked by the people they enslaved.[9]

Unfortunately, the 2017 incidents weren't the last of their kind. A year and a half later, on October 5, 2018, the Jewish community center was attacked again. Once again, its leaders immediately took up the grim task of power-washing more swastikas off its walls.

If hate and prejudice continue to find a voice in what once had been Ilda, however, it is drowned out on a regular basis by voices of faith in the area. Ilda never developed into a permanent community, but it has evolved into a home for a multitude of houses of worship. Within a mile on either side of Little River Turnpike from the crossroads are:

St. Ambrose Catholic
Little River United Church of Christ
St. Matthew's Methodist
Bethlehem Lutheran
Church of God of Prophecy
Providence Presbyterian
Chabad Lubavitz
Calvary Hill Baptist
City Gates Church
Highview Christian Fellowship
Calvary Church of the Nazarene

Residents of what was once Ilda now have myriad choices to worship, none of them restricted by race.

Standing Tall

It must have pained Dennis Howard to learn of the hateful incidents in the place his ancestors built out of nothing more than hope and dreams of a life of freedom and equality. In reality, of course, they were faced with racism—systemic, institutional, and personal—throughout their lives.

Howard endured his share of racism, too. But he, like Horace Gibson, Moses Parker, their children, and their descendants in the Pines of Merrifield, was a fighter. Whether in a junior high classroom, on a deployment with his army unit, or in a meeting with Virginia government officials, he did not shrink from a challenge and stood tall and strong in defense of his family, his heritage, and his convictions.

So it comes as something of a shock to learn that this literally larger-than-life figure died at the age of sixty-seven in 2018.

Howard is buried at Quantico National Cemetery, in Prince William County, Virginia. It's an altogether different place than Jermantown Cemetery, the Second Baptist Church graveyard, or the Sons and Daughters of Liberty Cemetery. There's no overgrowth. Every inch of the grounds is meticulously groomed, courtesy of the U.S. Department of Veterans Affairs. In one section, a sign reads, "Please excuse the appearance of this area while improvements are being made." But the surrounding grounds look immaculate.

There's no need to hunt for Howard's grave. It is carefully catalogued in a VA database, with specific directions and maps indicating its precise location. On an early spring day, the sun shines brightly over the gently rolling hills of the cemetery. In the distance, the hum of traffic on Interstate 95 can be heard, but other than that it's quiet and serene. A light, warm breeze freshens the air.

There's no mystery to this cemetery. It's not the size or scale of Arlington National Cemetery about thirty miles to the north, but it is imbued with the same overwhelming sense of sacrifice. Row upon row of simple white headstones, each one indicating someone who served their country, stretch out into the distance. They're identical except for the brief sentiments allowed at the bottom: "Loving Husband," "Big Daddy," "Smiling Blue Eyes," "Put Out to Sea, Dry Wit in Tow." Above, the names of the wars in which they served are etched: World War II, Korea, Vietnam, Persian Gulf, Iraq.

Howard's grave sits in the second row of one section of the cemetery. There's an opening in the row of stones in front of his, presumably to leave room for the roots of the tree that stands directly in front—a variety of pine, fittingly. But it also creates the impression that Howard was too imposing a presence to be contained by the standard grave.

His headstone is like new, sturdy and gleaming. There seems to be no doubt that it will be standing right here 150 years from now. It has a just-the-facts inscription: "Dennis E. Howard Jr., LTC, U.S. Army, Vietnam, Iraq, Jun 7 1950, Mar 13 2018, ARCOM." But the unstated message echoes Horace Gibson's headstone: Peace be thine.

Three years after Howard's death, the Guinea Road Cemetery once again got official recognition on a Virginia Department of Transportation map. A rectangular area on a 2021 map indicates its location with a dotted line marked "Cemetery (**See Note)." The note in question says that "all known graves have been relocated." The inclusion of the word "known" is a telling admission that there's no guarantee there aren't more graves under Guinea Road that were never found.[10]

VDOT created the map in connection with yet another construction project at the Little River Turnpike intersection, this time involving the right-turn lane on the opposite side of Guinea from where the graves were found in 2004. The project involved restriping the lane so drivers could have unimpeded access to the turnpike, and adding a pedestrian island to the north to make the intersection a little less harrowing for pedestrians.

The same issues that plagued the intersection for years led to the project: during the morning rush hour, VDOT determined, traffic backups more than sixty cars long developed on Guinea as drivers waited more than a minute and a half to turn right onto Little River.[11] That caused some commuters to use the side streets of the neighborhood to the east of Guinea Road as a cut-through. This was maddening to its residents. But those who lived on Guinea itself had a different perspective.

On March 1, 2021, VDOT held a virtual public information meeting in which area residents raised time-honored issues about the flow of traffic on Guinea Road. One, Greg Parnell, who said he lived one house away from the turnpike intersection, said, "For commuters, I think they see Guinea Road largely as a commuter artery. I think for those of us that live on and around Guinea Road it's important to remember that this is a residential road. There are houses on both sides of the street here, people that are living directly on this road, and my particular concern, my family's concern, is the lack of a sidewalk on the east side of Guinea Road around this area."[12] That proposal, VDOT said, was outside the scope of the project.

Fairfax County has made attempts to manage its growth over the years, but its basic position from the mid-twentieth century onward has been, "Let's welcome the people, the houses, and the cars, and somehow we'll figure out a way to deal with the infrastructure issues that causes." The Little River Turnpike–Guinea Road intersection is one place where this has played out for decades. And that's unlikely to change.

The Road to Reclamation

The Guinea Road Cemetery controversy was resolved to the satisfaction of all parties involved. That's often not the case. In 2003, Lynn Rainville, executive director of institutional history and museums at Washington and Lee University in Virginia, who has mapped African American cemeteries across the state, was asked to investigate the site of a former tavern in a small community called Morgantown near Charlottesville.

Oral tradition held that a cemetery for the enslaved was on the property.[13]

Rainville found eight fieldstones visible above the ground at the site, none of them inscribed with names or dates. The characteristics of the stones and the graveyard's location relative to the tavern suggested they marked the remains of people enslaved on the property. Local residents formed an association to try to block a construction company from disturbing the site to expand its operations. The company and county officials denied that the cemetery existed, citing the lack of inscriptions on the stones. The construction project was approved with slight modifications, despite an effort by the community association to solicit affidavits from African American residents to verify the oral history of the site.[14]

In the end, after all the controversy, the construction company decided to build its facility elsewhere.

There are many other similar stories, but in recent years, the success rate of efforts to preserve African American cemeteries is improving. There is "a quiet revolution taking place in Virginia and beyond," writes Ryan K. Smith in a 2020 study of Richmond's historic cemeteries: "Where white leaders long bolstered their heritage, authority, and sense of racial distinction with a corresponding disregard for the graves of others, the latter gravesites are presently inspiring widespread energies for their reclamation and preservation."[15]

Smith details efforts to preserve the African Burial Ground (previously known as the "Burying Ground for Negroes") in Richmond's Shockoe Bottom neighborhood. In the late 1990s, a researcher studying her family's history near the city determined that the cemetery was beneath a parking lot and part of Interstate 95. When Virginia Commonwealth University (VCU) purchased the parking lot for the use of its medical campus in 2007, state officials ordered an archaeological study of the property. As was the case initially with the Guinea Road Cemetery, it did not involve new excavations.

When VCU announced it would repave the lot, students and activists protested. Still, the university proceeded, leaving a fifty-foot patch of land unpaved for a memorial. Preservationists demanded more, and in 2011, the state purchased the site from VCU and gave it to the City of Richmond. Today, the burial ground has been reclaimed, with historical markers and stones to indicate its location.[16]

A second African Burial Ground in Richmond, though, provides a cautionary counterpoint to successful efforts to stave off development of burial grounds like that at Guinea Road. In the 1950s, city officials concluded that while they had been informed that records showed a piece of land that had been slated for development had long ago been reserved for use as a cemetery, "records fail to indicate whether it was ever used for the purposes for which it was designated." The site was sold to the Sun Oil Company, which built a gas station on it.[17]

In Northern Virginia and nearby regions of Maryland and the District of Columbia, concerns about preservation of African American cemeteries are taken more seriously now than they were a decade ago.

In 2014, the City of Alexandria, Virginia, dedicated a memorial to the Contrabands and Freedmen Cemetery, established during the Civil War as the last resting place for about 1,800 African Americans who fled their enslavers and took up residence in the city during the Civil War. The last recorded burial at the site took place in 1869, after which it fell victim to development. In 1955, a gas station was built on the site, and later an office building was added.[18]

The road to preserving the long-forgotten cemetery was a long one. In 1987, a historian noticed a reference to the cemetery in an 1894 edition of the *Alexandria Gazette,* which led to remote sensing efforts that indicated the presence of graves near gas pumps on the property. In the mid-1990s, activists pushed to preserve the cemetery, and it was rededicated in 2007.

Farther west, in Loudoun County, in 2015 the Rev. Michelle Thomas was looking for a piece of land on which to build a new church. She scoured county records to make sure that no location under consideration included a cemetery. In the process, she noticed references to the Belmont Slave Cemetery, named after the plantation on which it sat. She visited the cemetery, saw that it was in poor condition, and founded the Loudoun Freedom Center to work for its preservation.[19]

Two years later, real estate developer Toll Brothers Inc. donated 2.75 acres of land on which the cemetery lies to the Loudoun Freedom Center. It is now known as the African American Burial Ground for the Enslaved. In 2021, Toll Brothers agreed to transfer another four acres to the center, to be used to build replicas of buildings used by the enslaved.[20] Thomas has since expanded the center's work to include efforts to preserve other African American cemeteries in the region.

Cemetery preservation activists must not only be prepared for long battles with developers and government officials but also need to remain vigilant to make sure that even after African American graveyards are recognized, they remain protected.

Take the case of the Mount Zion–Female Union Band Society Historic Memorial Park, two adjoining cemeteries in Washington, D.C.'s Georgetown neighborhood. Together, they contain the remains of thousands of African Americans, both enslaved and free. In 2021, Lisa Fager, executive director of a foundation that works for the preservation of the cemeteries, was thunderstruck when she saw construction crews digging up a bike path that had been built on what had once been cemetery land. "Everyone keeps talking about these cemeteries that used to be," she told the *Washington Post*. "We're right here, right in front of your eyes, and we're falling apart. And no one is noticing."[21]

By late 2022, Congress had begun to notice. In December, lawmakers passed legislation creating an African American Burial Grounds Preservation Program in the National Park Service.[22] The law stated that Congress had found that "many African American burial grounds from before and after the Civil War are in a state of disrepair or inaccessibility due to overgrowth of vegetation, crumbling physical structures, and other challenges.... [E]stablishing a program to preserve previously abandoned, underserved, and other African-American burial grounds would help communities identify and record burial grounds and preserve local history, while better informing development decisions and community planning." But the law allotted only $3 million a year for the next five years to the Park Service to issue grants under the program—not nearly enough to address the thousands of identified and unidentified African American burial grounds nationwide.

Reckoning with History

When the Ilda historical marker was dedicated in 2010, it took its place along those commemorating Gooding's Tavern, John Mosby's exploits, and several dozen more in Fairfax County. But relatively few of the markers recognized African American sites of historical importance.

A decade later, as convulsive shocks around issues of race reverberated throughout the nation in the early 2020s, Fairfax County moved to change the way it preserves and interprets its history. The idea was both to honor the contributions of Black residents and to address sites and monuments memorializing Confederate figures. The county renamed several schools, and in November 2020 removed a monument to John Quincy Marr, the first Confederate soldier killed in the Civil War, from the grounds of the county courthouse.

Meanwhile, the Fairfax County History Commission was putting the finishing touches on a report ordered by the board of supervisors "listing a full inventory of Confederate street names, monuments and public places in Fairfax County and on Fairfax County-owned property." In early December 2021, the commission delivered its study. It was 539 pages long—and only included "generally known individuals," because "in many cases, there will be no means of verifying whether a common last name, i.e., Johnson, refers to a Confederate."[23]

The commission ended up examining 26,500 assets, painstakingly analyzing their heritage. Then it delivered its report to the board of supervisors to decide what to do with the data—including the dozens of streets and places named after Robert E. Lee and Stonewall Jackson alone.

The History Commission also created an African American History Inventory, including physical sites, collections, digital resources, oral histories, church and school histories, roadside markers, family records and objects.

In early 2022, the board of supervisors, Fairfax County Public Schools, the History Commission, and the county's Neighborhood and Community Services unit kicked off the Black/African American Experience Project. It included three elements: collecting stories, supporting project-based learning in schools, and erecting new historical markers focusing on African American people, events, and locations. Schools provided resources to help students uncover untold stories of Black county residents and groups, and then encouraged them to submit ideas for new markers. The county set up a website for African Americans to share their experiences. In September 2022, officials announced the county would erect six new historical markers highlighting key African American people and places.[24]

What Might Have Been

Ilda now occupies a place of pride in Fairfax County's Braddock District, which includes post–Civil War African American enclaves such as those around Methodist Zion Church (founded in 1876), Oak Hill Church (sometime before 1890), Little Zion Baptist Church (1895), and Radell Park Baptist Church (about 1900). It's likely that these communities, and possibly Ilda, too, included people once enslaved by the Fitzhughs, Goodings, and others.[25]

But while the other villages were made up exclusively of African Americans, Ilda was not. It was a racially integrated community that happened to be started by two African American families. And they weren't people who were working the land on which they had been enslaved. The Gibsons and Parkers moved to the county for the purpose of starting a new life.

They had a great deal of success, but their story, and Ilda's, is still one of what might have been. Not only did Ilda turn into a de facto whites-only community, but the descendants of its founders weren't even allowed to develop a thriving and lasting community in segregated Merrifield.

In the mid-1990s, in his book on the Gibson-Parker family legacy, Hareem Badil-Abish observed that Merrifield had become a hodgepodge of commercial operations lacking in character. "Our progenitors," he wrote, "would cringe at the sight of what has taken place to the community that once was ours through their toil, blood, and sacrifice."[26] At that time, Fairfax County residents lamented Merrifield's curious mix of older stores, industrial operations, a towering telecommunications apparatus, an aging movie multiplex, and an auto body repair shop covered in a garish mix of odd ornamentation. Amid this spectacle stood a working farm into the 1980s.

If Badil-Abish could see Merrifield today, he'd likely be appalled at how it has been turned into an even bigger monument to commercialization. At its center is the Mosaic District, the kind of suburban town center that caters to those with lots of disposable income. It is at once both inviting and disorienting. Rev. Dr. Paul Shepard, pastor of the First Baptist Church of Merrifield, recalls how the area changed during the nine years he was away from the county serving as pastor of a church in Savannah, Georgia.

"When I saw the Mosaic, I was stunned," he said. "I was stunned because number one, wow, they really developed. But I was also upset. Once again—this is commonplace in a Black community—meaning that at one time that community was predominantly Black, but what happened is, they developed around the Black church. But no one ever comes to the church and says, 'Listen, we are developing. We want to make it attractive. What can we do?' That has always been a pet peeve of mine: that you can build around instead of the church growing with the community in terms of aesthetics."[27]

Still, the Mosaic District vindicates Merrifield's history in one key way. Stroll through the artificial grass-covered green space at its heart on a warm evening, and you'll see ample evidence of what the region's white residents feared more than anything just a few decades earlier: a mix of people representing a vast number of different races and nationalities, their children running and playing together in that nonstop way that children do. Merrifield is far from being a color-blind community. But it is also far from the dystopia that fearful white residents promised if race-mixing and demographic change were allowed to proceed unchecked.

Few people in Fairfax County today are aware of the African American influence and experience in places like Ilda and Merrifield. In Ilda's case, if Hareem Badil-Abish and Dennis Howard hadn't fought to uncover their family's history and demanded that it be recognized, the community would have been lost to history. For more than two decades, they dug into records, interviewed relatives, examined family documents, and collected any other information they could find on Ilda. Then they spoke—loudly, clearly, and consistently over more than two decades—about the importance of preserving the Gibson-Parker legacy. Their work led directly to the discovery of the Guinea Road Cemetery. Amid the onslaught of development, successful efforts to address the concerns of descendants of those interred at such locations are rare. So give credit where it's due: government officials ultimately listened not only to Howard's reports of family oral tradition but to experts in locating cemeteries. When they found the Guinea Road Cemetery, they organized a respectful excavation of the remains found there.

Nevertheless, the fact is that the scales were tipped in favor of road construction and development from the beginning. That meant that the cemetery and all of the information it contained about the life and times of the people buried there—which was deemed important enough to make it eligible to be listed on the National Register of Historic Places—came perilously close to disappearing. There's no way of knowing how many cemeteries have suffered such a fate over the years in Fairfax County alone.

Without the effort to excavate the cemetery and relocate the remains found there, Ilda's story might have been lost forever. And it's more than just a tale of the rise and fall of a community. It exemplifies many of the key themes and trends that have shaped the history of the United States. Those include British colonialism, American independence, slavery, systemic racism, transportation, suburban development, faith and religion, preservation and memory. Understanding Ilda's rise and disappearance, and the fight to honor its legacy and its buried dead, leads to understanding a lot about the history of the United States and its current struggles, especially when it comes to issues of race. And odds are that the place formerly known as Ilda will continue to offer such lessons in the years to come.

The Ilda community wasn't someone's dream or a planned utopia. It was a place settled by two men and their families that held out the possibility of a better way of life to go with their newfound freedom. That they were denied the full fruits of that freedom only makes what they accomplished that much more impressive. They succeeded in business, property ownership, philanthropic work, faith development—and in launching a family legacy that has included successful business executives, teachers, lawyers, doctors, military service members, and more.

Ilda Lives

"There was a place they called Ilda, I'm telling you," insisted Everett Robey, an early twentieth-century resident of the area, in a 1982 interview. "It's not in existence any more."

Likewise, Douglas Dove, who also grew up nearby in the early 1900s, said in 1993, "I was born at a little place halfway between Annandale and Fairfax on Little River Turnpike. Little place called Ilda—I-L-D-A—just a wide place in the road."[28]

Today, virtually no physical traces of Ilda remain. Walking the length of it from east to west on the south side of Little River Turnpike, from Woodburn Road to Guinea Road, is a voyage into the heart of mundane suburbia. There, on your right, is CVS, near where the Ilda School stood. On the west side of Prosperity Avenue, nestled closely together, are Ariake Japanese Restaurant, a Shell gas station, a 7-Eleven, a dry cleaner, and a shuttered bank. Behind them looms a three-story Long & Foster realty office building. That's it for the commercial area.

Suburbia can have its own kind of quirky appeal. But there's no getting around it: this is charmless.

Across the street, just past a "Deer Crossing" sign (pity the poor doe or buck that would try to cross four lanes of fast-moving traffic here) is Dr. John Forest's home, where the Ilda Church once stood. It's a structure big enough to accommodate a good-sized house and adjoining dentist's office, but it's dwarfed by the latter-day mansion that now sits behind it.

Keep going and you'll pass through what was Richard Beach's property, south of the turnpike. Across the street was the black-smith shop, where Horace and Martha Gibson, Moses and Emily Parker, Page and Matilda Parker, and Robert Williams lived and worked. The Pozez Jewish Community Center of Northern Virginia and Station 23 of the Annandale Volunteer Fire Department now occupy much of this land.

Back on the other side of the turnpike, on the west side of Guinea Road, sits the piece of property where Franklin Minor once terrorized the neighborhood, and where a small cemetery became the final resting place for dozens of people, many of them enslaved or formerly enslaved.

With the multiple road-widening projects that have taken place over the years, only a small strip of underbrush and trees remains in the spot where the graveyard was. The rest has been claimed for the roadway and a sidewalk. On a midwinter's day, what's left of the vegetation is denuded. A small sign advertising "Windows/Siding/Trim/Roofing/Gutters" has blown over and sits on the grass. The large house behind the vegetation fits naturally on the lot now. It's doubtful anyone but longtime residents of the area are aware that this was once an overgrown vacant lot, much less a cemetery.

The roar and whine of fast-moving traffic is constant and unsettling. It's awkward and uncomfortable walking on the sidewalk, imparting the feeling one is doing something suspicious. Almost everyone around is in a car, and they're all going someplace else.

A boy on his way home from school teeters under the bulk of an enormous backpack, waiting an eternity for the traffic light to give him permission to cross Guinea Road. As he stands, cars lined up in the newly added right-turn lane on Guinea periodically honk their horns. They're irritated that the drivers ahead of them had the temerity to slow down, or even stop, before turning onto Little River Turnpike, instead of proceeding unabated through the intersection as intended. There's yet another road project of some sort underway, and work crews busy themselves removing road construction signs at the end of their workday.

Sitting on the base of a towering lamppost at the corner with the idea of listening for voices from deep below quickly feels both embarrassingly romantic and hopelessly futile. If such voices were shouting from the heavens, the insistent thrum of engine noise would drown them out. But to the right is visual evidence of their presence: a white wooden cross, placed at the base of the largest of a small stand of trees. Some unknown person first put a cross there after the cemetery was discovered. "For the dead buried here," it read. "R.I.P." That person, or perhaps someone else, has periodically replaced the cross with new versions ever since. By the spring of 2023, though, it was almost invisible, buried beneath a pile of downed tree limbs and underbrush.

The cross looks less like a cemetery marker and more like one of those makeshift roadside memorials to people killed in traffic accidents. But its presence is a sign of the opportunity for redemption that Ilda offers. It's a reminder of those who lived and died here without ever knowing the taste of freedom, those who sought to build a new life out of a still-unfulfilled promise of equality and opportunity, and those who insisted that this time, a historic resting place would not simply be paved over in the name of commuter convenience.

Ilda's story can be unearthed in historical documents, maps, letters, property deeds, newspaper clippings—and by literally digging. But that doesn't mean it's dead. Ilda lives in the legacy of Horace Gibson, Moses Parker, Hareem Badil-Abish, and Dennis Howard. It lives in the effort in Fairfax County to acknowledge,

A small cross near where the Guinea Road Cemetery was located honors the people who were buried there. (Photo by the author)

record, and understand the experiences of African Americans in its history. It lives in the spiritual work of the places of worship that now occupy what was once Ilda, and in the First Baptist Church of Merrifield. It lives in the Pozez Jewish Community Center and the Little River United Church of Christ, which shoulder the burden of being the targets of contemporary white supremacists carrying forward the sordid legacy of hate and bias that stunted the growth of Ilda. And it lives in the voices of the dead beneath Guinea Road, whether or not they can be heard.

Ilda lives, and speaks: Remember, it says. And do better.

ACKNOWLEDGMENTS

First, I must recognize my debt to the four central characters in the Ilda story: Horace Gibson, Moses Parker, Hareem Badil-Abish, and Dennis Howard. Their courage and tenacity in building a community and fighting to make sure its story was not erased from history—as so many others have been—inspired my efforts every step of the way.

My wife, Julie, not only provided support and encouragement for my work but read every word of the manuscript and asked the kind of probing questions about it that made me see the need for additional research and better organization and clarity in the writing. My marriage has put me in the fortunate position of being the second-best writer and editor in my own household. It has also given Julie and me two wonderful children, Molly and Kevin, with whom I was delighted to spend many happy hours as they grew up before considering taking up a project like this.

I cannot give enough thanks to Maddy McCoy, the most tenacious and mission-driven researcher I have ever encountered. She cut her teeth as a public historian on the Guinea Road cemetery investigation and since has built a career on digging up information that gives voice to the voiceless. On a hot summer's day in 2021, I stood with Maddy on the corner of Guinea Road and Little River Turnpike and said, "I'm going to write a book about this intersection." She shouted, "Yes!" when everyone else in the world would have said, "Huh?" Maddy trusted me with her time, her expertise, and her trove of documents on the Ilda area and the Guinea Road Cemetery. I hope I have delivered on the promise that I would use those resources wisely.

The archivists at the Fairfax County Circuit Court Historic Records Office, especially Georgia Brown, patiently and repeatedly walked me through the process of digging through Fairfax County land and court records. Then, as I floundered around, she went ahead and found the information for me. The staff at the office are wizards at conjuring up the past through records, maps, and deeds.

Joyce Bellamy, the historian of the First Baptist Church of Merrifield, provided an important perspective on the role of the Gibson-Parker descendants in its history and generously shared some of her own memories. She also connected me with Worthie Duckett, the sister of Hareem Badil-Abish.

Rev. Dr. Paul Shepard, pastor of First Baptist, related his experiences both as a young Black man growing up in Fairfax County and his current work of serving the church's still-active congregation.

The company where I worked as a journalist for more than thirty years, GovExec, gave me the opportunity to begin exploring the history of Ilda in an article called "The Plantation and the Pizza Hut" that I wrote for *Route Fifty*, a state and local government publication. Portions of this book first appeared in that article. My longtime GovExec colleague Katherine McIntire Peters reviewed the manuscript at an early stage and, with her keen eye for detail and historical analysis, provided very helpful feedback.

I feel like I know Brian Conley well, though I have only communicated with him via email. He not only worked tirelessly for years to uncover the story of Ilda and the Guinea Road Cemetery, but he also kept records of virtually every stage of the process. And he did something journalists only dream of—made sure they were publicly available in the Virginia Room of the City of Fairfax Regional Library.

The Virginia Room, an absolute treasure trove of historical information, became my second home during the research process. Chris Barbuschak and the staff there are incredibly patient and helpful in finding just what you're looking for, even when you're asking for cartloads of files at once.

Former Fairfax County Board of Supervisors chairman Sharon Bulova piqued my interest in the rich history of the area in which I live with her Look Back at Braddock project in 2004, resulting in the book *Braddock's True Gold*, which contained a number of oral histories, including an interview with Dennis Howard. James Walkinshaw, who holds the Braddock District supervisor seat that Bulova once occupied, inspired me to get started on this work with his video message about enslaved people at Oak Hill in 2020.

One of the coauthors of *Braddock's True Gold*, Mary Lipsey, was very helpful both in terms of the mountains of research she has done and in making connections with people who provided critical information about Ilda. I also greatly benefited from the exhaustive work done by the historians and researchers who have brought Fairfax County's rich history to life. Without the foundation laid by Beth Mitchell, Nan Netherton, D'Anne Evans, John Rutherford, John Browne, and so many more, this book simply would not have been possible. I'm also grateful to my fellow members of the Fairfax County History Commission, who have taught me so much about the county's historic heritage and efforts to preserve and protect it.

Brian Slawski and the members of Burke Historical Society allowed me to preview my research early on, providing encouragement and helping me to organize all the information I had gathered into what I hope is a coherent narrative.

At the University of Virginia Press, Nadine Zimmerli encouraged me to pursue this project and shepherded the manuscript—and me—through the review, revisions, and approval process in the middle of a raging pandemic. Her support from the very beginning meant the world to me. The two anonymous reviewers Nadine lined up to provide feedback on the manuscript offered keen insights and suggestions for further research that greatly improved the finished product. Mark Mones, head of Rivanna Books at UVA Press, carried the ball from there, and I'm grateful to him for publishing this book under the imprint. I also deeply appreciated the professionalism and care with which managing editor Ellen Satrom and copy editor Susan Murray handled the manuscript.

One of my oldest friends, Gregory Nemec, whose work as an illustrator has appeared in the *New York Times, Wall Street Journal, National Geographic Adventure,* and many other publications, produced the pair of illustrated maps of Ilda that are featured in the book. I chose to take as a compliment his comment that my sketches for the maps perfectly captured the amateurish touch that a nonprofessional would bring to the task of producing a map of their community.

Another old friend, Douglas Rife, was the first person I met who genuinely loved cemeteries. And as my boss at an educational publishing company early in my career, he gave me the opportunity to author a middle school history text that I lacked the credentials or experience to write. But it set me on my way as a writer and editor.

My father, Jim, a professional journalist for several decades (though he preferred the term "newspaperman"), taught me by example the importance of thorough, careful research and reporting. And he set a standard for clear, unadorned, engaging prose that I'm still trying to meet. My mother, Priscilla, also a trained journalist, immersed my brother, sisters, and me in the world of words when we were children by hauling us back and forth to the local branch of the Minneapolis Public Library, where we were in high heaven.

Throughout my work on this book, my adopted sister Nancy has served as my deepest inspiration. Through her eyes, I have caught a glimpse of the Black experience in America and also learned how easy it is to take one's privilege for granted even in your own family. Nancy's persistence in surmounting the myriad obstacles thrown in her way makes me proud to be her "brother from another mother."

In 1995, as Hareem Badil-Abish was putting the finishing touches on the draft of his family history, he noted that "this project has increased in complexity and range as I continually uncovered important facts and information regarding my family as well as other Black families in and around Fairfax County." He concluded that "much more research and documentation is needed. This work is only the beginning."[1]

Ten years later, at a low point in Dennis Howard's quest to convince government officials at the county and state levels in Virginia to recognize that an African American cemetery existed at the crossroads of what had been Ilda, he wrote to Brian Conley in frustration. The way things were headed, he argued, "a generation from now when we are all dead and gone, no one will know who lived and died on the Little River Turnpike at Guinea Road."[2]

If I have helped in a small way to continue the work Hareem Badil-Abish said was so badly needed, and to ensure that Dennis Howard's fears are not realized, then I have accomplished what I set out to do in writing this book.

NOTES

Introduction

1. "A Dastardly Crime," *Richmond Planet*, October 8, 1898, 1.
2. "Possible Threats against Road Project Investigated," WTOPnews
   .com, June 29, 2007, Guinea Road Cemetery file, Virginia Room,
   City of Fairfax Regional Library.
3. Virginia Department of Transportation, "Under Construction:
   Little River Turnpike and Guinea Road Intersection Improvements in Fairfax County," June 25, 2021, https://www.virginiadot
   .org/projects/northern-virginia/littleriverguinea.asp.
4. Emily Williams, *Stories in Stone* (Wilmington, DE: Vernon, 2020), 5.

1. Destruction

1. Fairfax County Comprehensive Plan, 1991, 53, https://www
   .fairfaxcounty.gov/planning-development/sites/planning
   -development/files/assets/documents/comprehensiveplan
   /planhistoric/1995/area2/fairfax.pdf.
2. Fairfax Harrison, *Landmarks of Old Prince William* (Richmond,
   VA: Old Dominion Press, 1924), 25, 33.
3. Nan Netherton, Donald Sweig, Janice Artemel, Patricia Hinkin,
   and Patrick Reed, *Fairfax County, Virginia: A History* (Fairfax, VA:
   Fairfax County Board of Supervisors, 1978), 31–32.
4. Netherton et al. *Fairfax County, Virginia: A History*, 35.

5. Sharon Bulova, interview by the author, August 13, 2021.

6. Historic Oak Hill Virtual Visit, Fairfax County Parks Authority, November 1, 2020, YouTube, https://www.youtube.com/watch?v=3AxubZ1K3kk.

7. John Browne, appearance on video program *Virginia Time Travel*, September 13, 2018, https://www.youtube.com/watch?v=Pma2nYzvBYs.

8. Micki McElya, *The Politics of Mourning: Death and Honor in Arlington National Cemetery* (Cambridge, MA: Harvard University Press, 2016), 13.

9. Edward Howrey, *Washington Lawyer* (Iowa City: University of Iowa College of Law, 1983), 155.

10. Patricia Marshall, "The Ghost of Oak Hill" (in box of papers donated by D'Anne Evans related to her book *Wakefield Chapel*), Virginia Room, City of Fairfax Regional Library, January 29, 1963.

11. James Walkinshaw, interview by the author, August 6, 2021.

12. Sharon Bulova, interview by the author, August 13, 2021.

13. Maddy McCoy, interview by the author, January 21, 2022.

14. Fairfax Circuit Court Minute Book, 1807, 30.

15. *Industrial Sketch of Fairfax County, Virginia* (Fairfax, VA: Fairfax County Board of Supervisors, 1907), 90.

16. "Sideburn," *Fairfax Herald*, August 8, 1919, 2.

17. "Guinea Road Not Always a Straight Shot," *Burke Connection*, November 19, 2002.

18. User comment on Fairfax Underground, May 9, 2011, http://www.fairfaxunderground.com/forum/.

19. Mechal Sobel, *The World They Made Together: Black and White Values in Eighteenth-Century Virginia* (Princeton, NJ: Princeton University Press, 1987), 3.

20. John Chester Miller, *The Wolf by the Ears: Thomas Jefferson and Slavery* (New York: Free Press, 1977), 240.

21. Edward Ball, "Retracing Slavery's Trail of Tears," *Smithsonian*, November 2015, https://www.smithsonianmag.com/history/slavery-trail-of-tears-180956968/.

22. Sobel, *The World They Made Together*, 93–94.

23. "Our Historic Home in Annandale," Pleasant Valley Memorial Park website, https://www.dignitymemorial.com/funeral-homes/virginia/annandale/pleasant-valley-memorial-park/0598.

24. "Slave History near LRUCC," Little River United Church of Christ website, 1, https://static1.squarespace.com/static/5a4c0633914e6b17448f8f17/t/5aeb6622562fa7a9b2481c07/1525376547915/slaveHistoryNearLRUCC.pdf.

25. Michael S. Mitchell, "Oak Hill Kitchen Skirmish," https://braddockheritage.org/archive/files/71c320a6c3dc8b1f64bda609b2ba380c.pdf.

26. United States War Department, *The War of the Rebellion: A Compilation of the Official Records of the Union and Confederate Armies* (Washington, DC: US Government Printing Office, 1880–1901), 80.

27. John Milner Associates, Inc., *Fairfax County Civil War Sites Inventory* (Fairfax, VA: Fairfax County Park Authority, August 2002), https://www.fairfaxcounty.gov/parks/sites/parks/files/assets /documents/naturalcultural/civil%20war%20inventory.pdf.

28. J. T. Trowbridge, *A Picture of the Desolated States and the Work of Restoration, 1865–1868* (Hartford, CT: L. Stebbins, 1868).

29. Netherton et al. *Fairfax County, Virginia: A History*, 395.

2. Reconstruction

1. *All Not So Quiet along the Potomac: The Civil War in Northern Virginia & Beyond*, blog, March 31, 2011, http:// dclawyeronthecivilwar.blogspot.com/.

2. Hareem Badil-Abish, *Shades of Gray: A Beginning . . . The Origins and Development of a Black Family in Virginia* (Estate of Hareem Badil-Abish, 2005), 34.

3. Maddy McCoy, interview by the author, January 21, 2022.

4. Badil-Abish, *Shades of Gray*, 35.

5. John Henderson Russell, "The Free Negro in Virginia 1619–1865" (PhD diss., Johns Hopkins University, 1913), 98.

6. Russell, "The Free Negro in Virginia 1619–1865," 98–99.

7. Russell, "The Free Negro in Virginia 1619–1865," 107.

8. Office of Comprehensive Planning, Fairfax County, *Fairfax Chronicles, A History and Historic Preservation Newsletter* 1, no. 3 (Summer 1977).

9. "Fairfax County Court," *Alexandria Gazette*, September 29, 1855.

10. Nan Netherton, Donald Sweig, Janice Artemel, Patricia Hinkin, and Patrick Reed, *Fairfax County, Virginia: A History* (Fairfax, VA: Fairfax County Board of Supervisors, 1978), 270.

11. Russell, "The Free Negro in Virginia 1619–1865," 115–16.

12. Netherton et al., *Fairfax County, Virginia: A History*, 258–59.

13. Ira Berlin, *Slaves without Masters: The Free Negro in the Antebellum South* (New York: New Press, 2007), 352.

14. Netherton et al., *Fairfax County, Virginia: A History*, 255, 265.

15. Maddy McCoy, Slavery Inventory Database, https://slavery inventorydatabase.com/.

16. Badil-Abish, *Shades of Gray*, 52–55.

17. Badil-Abish, *Shades of Gray*, 51.

18. U.S. Census, 1870.

19. Fairfax County Deed Book P4–506, April 12, 1869.

20. Fairfax County Will Book G2:36.
21. Fairfax County Chancery Court Records, March 1866.
22. *Alexandria Gazette*, December 13, 1865, 3.
23. Fairfax County Chancery Court Records, March 1866.
24. Curtis L. Vaughn, *Freedom Is Not Enough: African Americans in Antebellum Fairfax County* (PhD diss., George Mason University, 2008), 83.
25. Fairfax County Circuit Court Minute Books, 1863–1867, 65.
26. Louis Berger Group Inc., *Data Recovery at Guinea Road Cemetery Site (Site 44FX1664) Route 236 (Little River Turnpike)* (Richmond: Virginia Department of Transportation, March 2009), 2.
27. Debbie Robison, "List of Blacks in Fairfax County, VA, 1866–69, Based on Personal Property Tax Records," Northern Virginia History Notes website, http://www.novahistory.org/Fairfax _Blacks_1866-1869/Fairfax_Blacks_1866-1869.htm.
28. Fairfax County Personal Property Tax Records, 1862–1870.
29. Dennis Howard, oral history interview by Mary Lipsey, August 15, 2005, https://braddockheritage.org/archive/files /d6774c756c4445e9548d89809ec6db03.pdf.
30. Badil-Abish, *Shades of Gray*, 38.
31. G. M. Hopkins, *Atlas of 15 Miles around Washington, D.C.* (Philadelphia: G. M. Hopkins), 1878.
32. Fairfax County Circuit Court Historic Records.
33. *Washington Star*, September 11, 1877, 4.
34. "Board Supervisors: Some Few Minor Road Matters Taken up and Acted Upon," *Fairfax Herald*, August 9, 1929, 1.
35. Andrew M. D. Wolf, *Black Settlement in Fairfax County during Reconstruction*, research study (Fairfax, VA: Fairfax County Office of Comprehensive Planning, 1975), 63.
36. Louis Berger Group Inc., *Data Recovery at Guinea Road Cemetery Site*, 23.
37. Fairfax County Personal Property Tax Records, 1862–1870.
38. Brian A. Conley, *Return to Union: Fairfax County's Role in the Adoption of the Virginia Constitution of 1870* (Fairfax, VA: Fairfax County Public Library, 2001).
39. Badil-Abish, *Shades of Gray*, 19.
40. "A Place in Virginia Called Gum Springs," *New York Times*, November 9, 1986, A26, https://www.nytimes.com/1985/11/08/us /a-place-in-virginia-called-gum-springs.html.
41. "Protest over Road Widening through Black Community Stirs Memories of a Similar Fight in 1967," *Washington Post*, September 12, 2021, https://www.washingtonpost.com/transportation /2021/09/12/gum-springs-richmond-highway-virginia/.
42. Netherton et al., *Fairfax County, Virginia: A History*, 409.
43. Howard, oral history interview by Lipsey.

44. Netherton et al., *Fairfax County, Virginia: A History,* 447.

45. Netherton et al., *Fairfax County, Virginia: A History,* 445.

46. "Farmers' Bulletin," U.S. War Department, December 27, 1877, accessed via https://www.abaa.org/.

47. *Fairfax Herald,* December 24, 1886, referenced in "News of 75 Years Ago," *Fairfax Herald,* December 22, 1961.

48. Fairfax County Circuit Court Historic Records.

49. Badil-Abish, *Shades of Gray,* 56.

50. Louis Berger Group Inc., *Data Recovery at Guinea Road Cemetery Site,* 26.

51. 1880 U.S. Census, accessed via Ancestry.com.

52. William Page Johnson, *Brothers and Cousins: Confederate Soldiers and Sailors of Fairfax County, Virginia* (Athens, GA: Iberian Publishing, 1995), 13.

53. Pvt. Richard Watson Beach memorial, https://www.findagrave.com/memorial/6573994/richard-watson-beach.

3. Transition

1. Fairfax County Deed Book Liber Q, No. 4, 449.

2. Tiffany Stanley, "The Disappearance of a Distinctively Black Way to Mourn," *Atlantic,* January 26, 2016, https://www.theatlantic.com/business/archive/2016/01/black-funeral-homes-mourning/426807/.

3. Ross W. Jamieson, "Material Culture and Social Death: African-American Burial Practices," *Historical Archaeology* 29, no. 4 (1995): 39–58, http://www.jstor.org/stable/25616423.

4. Ira Berlin, *Slaves without Masters: The Free Negro in the Antebellum South* (New York: New Press, 2007), 306–7.

5. Lynn Rainville, *Hidden History: African American Cemeteries in Central Virginia* (Charlottesville: University of Virginia Press, 2014), 56.

6. Rainville, *Hidden History,* 62.

7. "Cemetery's History," City of Fairfax website, https://www.fairfaxva.gov/government/public-works/operations-division/cemetery/cemetery-s-history.

8. Fairfax County Deed Book I4–429.

9. Fairfax County Circuit Court Minute Book, 1860–1880, 226.

10. Rainville, *Hidden History,* 62.

11. John Kelly, "Preparing for the Future by Honoring the Past," *Washington Post,* April 27, 2006, B3.

12. *Fairfax Herald,* March 27, 1908, quoted in D'Anne A. Evans, *Wakefield Chapel* (Fairfax, VA: Fairfax County Office of Comprehensive Planning, 1977), 41.

13. Louis Berger Group Inc., *Data Recovery at Guinea Road Cemetery Site (Site 44FX1664) Route 236 (Little River Turnpike)* (Richmond: Virginia Department of Transportation, March 2009), 129–30.
14. All references to court proceedings are from *Commonwealth of Virginia v. Minor*, Fairfax Circuit Court Term Papers, 1880-051, May 1880.
15. Fairfax County Deeds, Liber Book 4673, 132.
16. Fairfax County Board of Zoning Appeals, Minute Book 22, November 7, 1978, 466.
17. "The Church at Ilda," *Fairfax Herald*, June 28, 1907, 3.
18. "The Church at Ilda," *Fairfax Herald*, October 4, 1907, 3.
19. "From Washington," *Alexandria Gazette*, October 6, 1893, 2.
20. "Ilda-Wakefield," *Fairfax Herald*, March 13, 1908, 3.
21. "Ilda," *Fairfax Herald*, August 14, 1914, 3.
22. Marion Dobbins, "Freedmen of Northern Virginia: Independence through Landownership, Black Communities and the Northern Virginia Baptist Association," paper for "History 711" class, George Mason University, May 12, 2014, https://www.academia.edu/8153029/Freedmen_of_Northern_Virginia_Black_communities_and_the_Northern_Virginia_Baptist_Association.
23. "The History of Second Baptist Church," Second Baptist Church of Falls Church website, https://sbcfallschurch.org/history/.
24. Badil-Abish, *Shades of Gray: A Beginning . . . The Origins and Development of a Black Family in Virginia* (Estate of Hareem Badil-Abish, 2005), 65.
25. Greater Merrifield Business Association website, https://www.greatermerrifield.org/.
26. Everett Robey, oral history interview by Jennifer Santley, deposited at Northern Virginia Folklife Center, George Mason University, 1981–82.
27. Rev. Dr. Paul Shepard, interview by the author, January 20, 2022.
28. Roosevelt Der Tatevasion, "Merrifield: Postscript to Civil War," *Fairfax County Sun-Echo*, April 19, 1962, 6.
29. Jeff Clark (Office of Communications and Community Relations, Fairfax County Public Schools), interview by the author, February 21, 2023.
30. Naomi Sokol Zeavin and Fairfax County History Commission, comps., "African American History in Mason District" (Fairfax, VA: Fairfax County History Commission, 2005).
31. Badil-Abish, *Shades of Gray*, 94.
32. *Fairfax Herald*, October 13, 1905, and November 10, 1905, quoted in Nan Netherton, Donald Sweig, Janice Artemel, Patricia Hinkin, and Patrick Reed, *Fairfax County, Virginia: A History* (Fairfax, VA: Fairfax County Board of Supervisors, 1978), 472.

33. Falls Church District School Board Minutes, 1887–1921, https://www.fcps.edu/sites/default/files/media/pdf/Falls%20Church%20District%20School%20Board%20Minutes%201897-1921.pdf.

34. Entry for "Ilda School" in appendix to K. S. Hogan, *Centennial Chronicle of Fairfax County Public Schools, Commonwealth of Virginia, 1870–1970* (n.d.).

35. Falls Church District School Board Minutes, 1887–1921.

36. Robey, oral history by Santley.

37. Fairfax County School Board Minutes, February 6, 1951, and October 7, 1952.

38. Fairfax County School Board Minutes, February 6, 1951, and October 7, 1952.

39. "School History," Wakefield Forest Elementary School website, https://wakefieldforestes.fcps.edu/about.

40. "Our Beliefs," Wakefield Forest Elementary School website, https://wakefieldforestes.fcps.edu/about.

41. Netherton et al., *Fairfax County, Virginia: A History*, 461.

42. "Local Brevities," *Alexandria Gazette*, May 20, 1910, 3.

43. "Fairfax Notes," *Alexandria Gazette*, November 20, 1896, 2.

44. "Trustees' Sale of Valuable Improved Real Estate," *Fairfax Herald*, April 5, 1912, 2.

45. Information about Gibson and Parker family members from Badil-Abish, *Shades of Gray*, 40–57.

46. Netherton et al., *Fairfax County, Virginia: A History*, 458.

47. Netherton et al., *Fairfax County, Virginia: A History*, 469.

48. Netherton et al., *Fairfax County, Virginia: A History*, 470.

49. *Industrial and Historical Sketch of Fairfax County* (Fairfax, VA: Fairfax County Board of Supervisors, 1907), https://archive.org/details/industrialhistor00fair/page/n7/mode/2up.

50. "A Dastardly Crime," *Richmond Planet*, October 8, 1898, 1.

51. *Alexandria Gazette*, October 18, 1898, 3.

52. "Local Brevities," *Alexandria Gazette*, March 6, 1899, 3.

53. "His Hip Pocket Was Loaded," *Washington Post*, October 25, 1899, 2.

54. "Franklin Minor Committed to Asylum," *Washington Post*, December 2, 1899, 12.

55. Badil-Abish, *Shades of Gray*, 38.

4. Segregation

1. *Fairfax Herald*, March 30, 1923, quoted in Nan Netherton, Donald Sweig, Janice Artemel, Patricia Hinkin, and Patrick Reed, *Fairfax County, Virginia: A History* (Fairfax, VA: Fairfax County Board of Supervisors, 1978), 534.

2. Netherton et al., *Fairfax County, Virginia: A History*, 666.

3. Netherton et al., *Fairfax County, Virginia: A History*, 536.

4. Netherton et al, *Fairfax County, Virginia: A History*, 404.

5. Netherton et al., *Fairfax County, Virginia: A History*, 540–41.

6. D. Anne A. Evans, *Wakefield Chapel* (Fairfax, VA: Fairfax County Office of Comprehensive Planning, 1977), 55.

7. "Former Pastor Dead," *Fairfax Herald*, August 28, 1925, 5.

8. Lowell T. Wakefield, oral history interview by D'Anne Evans, December 9, 1976.

9. "Aunt Martha Dead," *Fairfax Herald*, October 22, 1926, 5.

10. "Strother Gibson Dead," *Fairfax Herald*, April 22, 1927, 5.

11. William A. West, oral history interview by C. J. S. Durham and Mrs. Charles Rieger for the Fairfax County History Commission, September 17, 1974.

12. Printed in William Page Johnson, *Brothers and Cousins: Confederate Soldiers and Sailors of Fairfax County, Virginia* (Athens, GA: Iberian Publishing, 1995), viii.

13. "Death of Aged Colored Woman," *Fairfax Herald*, February 27, 1942, 1.

14. Edward T. Folliard, "Dixie Rides Again, Flying Its Battle Flag of the Confederacy," *Washington Post*, November 13, 1951, B1.

15. Netherton et al., *Fairfax County, Virginia: A History*, 544–45.

16. United States Department of Agriculture Bureau of Public Roads and Ford Motor Company, *The Road to Happiness*, film, 1924, https://www.youtube.com/watch?v=NZnuo0ZftAc.

17. "Little River Pike Project Delayed," *Washington Post*, May 19, 1922, 9.

18. Russ Banham, *The Fight for Fairfax* (Fairfax, VA: George Mason University Press, 2020), 11.

19. "Fairfax Board Gets Road Work Budget," *Washington Post*, October 23, 1932, M14.

20. "Bruen Chapel to Honor Golden Anniversary," *Northern Virginia Sun*, March 25, 1972, 4.

21. S. Fayette Cartledge, "Norfolk Combines Store, Service Sta.," *Fairfax Herald*, June 2, 1933, 3.

22. "Ilda, Va., Working for Electric Lights," *Herndon Observer*, January 29, 1925, 5.

23. *Annual Report of the Fairfax County Health Unit for the Year 1935*, quoted in Harry Hunter Burks Jr., "The Development of the Public Elementary School System of Fairfax County, Virginia from the School Year 1927–28 through the School Year 1941–42" (master's thesis in education, Duke University, 1942).

24. "Will Open Quarry," *Fairfax Herald*, October 24, 1930, 1.

25. "U.D.C. Meeting," *Fairfax Herald*, February 12, 1937, 1.

26. "Fairfax 'Bean Rain' Is Solved by Doerr," *Washington Post*, November 29, 1930, 4.

27. Fairfax County Board of Supervisors Meeting Minutes, April 6, 1938.
28. Edward Howrey, *Washington Lawyer* (Iowa City: University of Iowa College of Law, 1983), 126.
29. D. Anne A. Evans, *Wakefield Chapel* (Fairfax, VA: Fairfax County Office of Comprehensive Planning, 1977).
30. "Soldiers Accused of Starting Fight," *Washington Post*, August 24, 1931, 2.
31. "Fairfax Crusades on Dance Hall Rum," *Washington Post*, April 25, 1932, 5.
32. "Priest Is Fined $50 in Rum Possession," *Washington Post*, May 20, 1932, 7.
33. "Commissioners' Sale of Valuable Real Estate," *Fairfax Herald*, June 3, 1932, 5.
34. Fairfax County Board of Zoning Appeals, Minute Book 1, October 26, 1942, 116.
35. Fairfax County Board of Zoning Appeals, Minute Book 1, July 21, 1941, 13.
36. Marion Meany and Mary Lipsey, *Braddock's True Gold: 20th Century Life in the Heart of Fairfax County* (Fairfax, VA: County of Fairfax, 2007), 69.
37. *Fairfax Herald*, November 10, 1944, 1.
38. Meany and Lipsey, *Braddock's True Gold*, 74.
39. Banham, *The Fight for Fairfax*, 13.
40. Burks, "The Development of the Public Elementary School System of Fairfax County, Virginia from the School Year 1927–28 through the School Year 1941–42."
41. Fairfax County Board of Zoning Appeals, Minute Book 2, March 15, 1949, 60.
42. Fairfax County Historical Imagery Viewer, https://www.fairfaxcounty.gov/maps/aerial-photography.
43. Fairfax County Board of Zoning Appeals, Minute Book 3, September 16, 1952, 74.
44. Fairfax County Board of Zoning Appeals, Minute Book 2, April 3, 1951, 311.
45. *Fairfax Herald*, March 18, 1955, 6.
46. *Washington Post*, February 15, 1953, R2, quoted in Banham, *The Fight for Fairfax*, 21.
47. Jean Packard, oral history interview by Margaret Shuler, May 2, 2005.
48. Fairfax County Board of Zoning Appeals, Minute Book 12, September 13, 1966, 202.
49. *Citizen's Handbook of Fairfax County*, 1964, introductory message.
50. Image of newspaper article published in Meany and Lipsey, *Braddock's True Gold*, 77.

51. "Dulles Airport Has Its Roots in Rural Black Community of Willard," *Washington Post,* November 17, 2002.

52. *Pine Ridge Park: Master Plan Amendment* (Fairfax, VA: Fairfax County Park Authority, September 26, 2007, 5), https://www .fairfaxcounty.gov/sites/parks/files/assets/documents/plandev /master-plans/pineridge_mp_v2.pdf.

53. Avonjeannette "Dolly" Hill, oral history interview by Naomi Sokol Zeavin, 2005; Naomi Sokol Zeavin and Fairfax County History Commission, comps., "African American History in Mason District" (Fairfax, VA: Fairfax County History Commission, 2005).

54. Marion Dobbins, oral history interview by Linda Byrne for the Providence District History Project, January 21, 2008.

55. Aileen Wright, oral history interview by Mary Lipsey for the Providence District History Project, October 25, 2007.

56. Jacqueline L. Salmon, "Park's Allure Hides Pain of Past," *Washington Post,* April 14, 2000, A1

57. Eric Lipton, "Debate over the Future of Pine Ridge," *Washington Post,* June 26, 1997, VA1B.

58. Jacqueline L. Salmon, "Park's Allure Hides Pain of Past," *Washington Post,* April 14, 2000, A1.

59. Wright, interview by Lipsey.

60. "Two Groups of Houses Are Announced," *Washington Star,* August 4, 1951, 25.

61. Advertisement in *Washington Star,* July 19, 1952, 27.

62. Deed of Dedication, Lee Forest subdivision, Fairfax County Deed Book 743, p. 346, February 11, 1950.

63. "Delinquent Tax List, Fairfax County, Virginia: Providence District," *Fairfax Herald,* March 9, 1956.

64. Fairfax County Board of Zoning Appeals, Minute Book 22, March 14, 1978, 145–46.

65. Fairfax County Planning Commission Meeting Minutes, June 8, 1983.

5. Determination

1. Beryl Dill Kneen, "Bethlehem Church off to Good Start," *Northern Virginia Sun,* April 15, 1963, 2.

2. Aileen Wright, oral history interview by Mary Lipsey for the Providence District History Project, October 25, 2007.

3. Judge James Keith, oral history interview by Karen Coleman, March 11, 1974, Virginia Room, Fairfax City Regional Library.

4. *Washington Post,* September 20, 1959, B1.

5. "Statement, Superintendent Woodson Opposes Desegregation," July 6, 1959, Fairfax County Public Schools website, https://www

.fcps.edu/about-fcps/history/records/desegregation/writings #1959-woodson.

6. John Lawson, "Parents Irate at Fairfax Plan to Shift Pupils," *Washington Star*, February 7, 1962, C2.

7. Publisher's note in Hareem Badil-Abish, *Shades of Gray: A Beginning . . . The Origins and Development of a Black Family in Virginia* (Estate of Hareem Badil-Abish, 2005).

8. Dennis Howard, oral history interview by Mary Lipsey, August 15, 2005, https://braddockheritage.org/archive/files /d6774c756c4445e9548d89809ec6db03.pdf.

9. Howard, oral history interview by Lipsey.

10. Dennis Howard, oral history interview by Ira Andrews, Macon Memories Oral History Project, Randolph-Macon College, 2008, https://www.youtube.com/watch?v=NsjQYD8IFL4.

11. Howard, oral history interview by Lipsey.

12. Hareem Badil-Abish to Dennis Howard, February 1, 1993, included in Badil-Abish, *Shades of Gray*, 2.

13. Publisher's note in Badil-Abish, *Shades of Gray*.

14. Biographical information about Hareem Badil-Abish from pamphlet distributed at his memorial service, December 6, 1997, included in Guinea Road Cemetery file, Virginia Room, Fairfax City Regional Library.

15. Judge James Keith, oral history interview by Mary Lipsey, August 15, 2005, Virginia Room, Fairfax City Regional Library.

16. Nan Netherton, Donald Sweig, Janice Artemel, Patricia Hinkin, and Patrick Reed, *Fairfax County, Virginia: A History* (Fairfax, VA: Fairfax County Board of Supervisors, 1978), 664.

17. *A County Called Fairfax: Being a Student's Digest of Our Government and History* (Fairfax, VA: Fairfax County Office of the County Executive, 1966).

18. Garrett Epps, "Want to Know More about Critical Race Theory? Look at Virginia's Schools—For More Than 75 Years," *Washington Monthly*, October 25, 2021, https://washingtonmonthly.com/2021 /10/25/want-to-know-more-about-critical-race-theory-look-at -virginias schools-for-more-than-75-years/.

19. Fairfax County Cemetery Survey website, https://www.fairfax county.gov/library_cemeteries/Cemetery.aspx?number=FX187.

20. Marion Meany and Mary Lipsey, *Braddock's True Gold: 20th Century Life in the Heart of Fairfax County* (Fairfax, VA: County of Fairfax, 2006), v.

21. Cheryl Anderson, "Things I Remember from the Early Days Living on Guinea Rd.," Little Run Civic Association website, https:// www.lrcaonline.org/.

22. Ross Banham, *The Fight for Fairfax* (Fairfax, VA: George Mason University Press, 2020), 107, 110.

23. Quoted in Banham, *The Fight for Fairfax*, 108, 109.
24. Banham, *The Fight for Fairfax*, 126.
25. Quoted in Banham, *The Fight for Fairfax*, 130.
26. Banham, *The Fight for Fairfax*, 97.
27. *Washington Star*, November 19, 1979, 59, and December 12, 1979, 62.
28. "History of Pozez JCC of Northern Virginia," Pozez JCC website, https://www.thej.org/about/about/.
29. Patricia Davis, "N. Virginia Jewish Center Vandalized," *Washington Post*, December 2, 1993, D1.
30. Marylou Tousignant, "Bias Forum Disrupted by Threats," *Washington Post*, December 9, 1993, C1.
31. Netherton et al., *Fairfax County, Virginia: A History*, 653–55.
32. Records of meeting of Fairfax County Planning Commission, June 8, 1983.
33. Ron Shaffer, "The High Risks of Hot Pursuit," *Washington Post*, February 18, 1993, VA-4.
34. Kenneth Bredemeier, "Word on the Street: County Targets Ads," *Washington Post*, July 5, 2001, VA-4.

6. Revelation

1. Eric Lipton, "A Man with a Grave Mission," *Washington Post*, April 30, 1995, 31.
2. Susan L. Henry, "Fairfax County Archaeology Preliminary Site Survey Report: Guinea Road Cemetery," Heritage Resources, Fairfax County Office of Comprehensive Planning, August 1989.
3. Suzanne Levy, quoted in Lipton, "A Man with a Grave Mission," 31.
4. Kay R. McCarron, *An Archaeological Review of the Mondan Tract at the Intersection of Guinea Road and Little River Turnpike, Fairfax County Virginia*, July 31, 1990, 1.
5. "Winner's a Symbol of the New South," *Washington Star*, June 12, 1968, B-4.
6. Notes from Donald Schudel interview by Maddy McCoy, February 2008, courtesy Maddy McCoy.
7. Notes from Donald Schudel interview by Maddy McCoy, February 2008, courtesy Maddy McCoy.
8. Andy Williams, "Guinea Road/Little River Turnpike" article draft.
9. Fairfax County Zoning Evaluation Division Staff Report, Application RZ 89-A-081, November 21, 1990, 3.
10. McCarron, *An Archaeological Review of the Mondan Tract*, appendix.
11. McCarron, *An Archaeological Review of the Mondan Tract*, 2.

12. Louis Berger Group Inc., *Data Recovery at Guinea Road Cemetery Site (Site 44FX1664) Route 236 (Little River Turnpike)* (Richmond: Virginia Department of Transportation, March 2009), 132.
13. Brian Conley to Andy Williams, November 6, 2004, personal files of Maddy McCoy.
14. Brian Conley to Hareem Badil-Abish, November 14, 1990, personal files of Maddy McCoy.
15. Larry Moore, memorandum to Kris Abrahamson, November 14, 1990, Guinea Road Cemetery file, Virginia Room, City of Fairfax Regional Library.
16. Fairfax County Zoning Evaluation Division Staff Report, Application RZ 89-A-081, November 21, 1990, 4, 7.
17. Douglas Owsley, Report of Survey, Archaeological Site 44FX1664, June 20, 1991.
18. Hareem Badil-Abish to Brian Conley, March 23, 1995, faxed letter, Guinea Road Cemetery file, Virginia Room, Fairfax City Regional Library.
19. Brian Conley to Hareem Badil-Abish, March 23, 1995, Guinea Road Cemetery file, Virginia Room, Fairfax City Regional Library.
20. Dennis Howard to James S. Gilmore, April 21, 2000, Guinea Road Cemetery file, Virginia Room, Fairfax City Regional Library.
21. Dennis Howard to Brian Conley, May 8, 2000, Guinea Road Cemetery file, Virginia Room, Fairfax City Regional Library.
22. John Kelly, "What Lies Beneath," *Washington Post*, April 7, 2004, C12.
23. Kelly, "What Lies Beneath," C12.
24. Kelly, "What Lies Beneath," C12.
25. Andy Williams, "Guinea Road/Little River Turnpike Cemetery," article prepared for *VLTA Examiner*, a publication of the Virginia Land Title Association, July 20, 2005, Guinea Road Cemetery file, Virginia Room, Fairfax City Regional Library.
26. Andrew Williams to Dennis Howard, March 25, 2004, Guinea Road Cemetery file, Virginia Room, Fairfax City Regional Library.
27. Dennis Howard to Andrew Williams, March 27, 2004, Guinea Road Cemetery file, Virginia Room, Fairfax City Regional Library.
28. Dennis Howard to Gibson-Parker Family Members, March 27, 2004, Guinea Road Cemetery file, Virginia Room, Fairfax City Regional Library.
29. Dennis Howard to Brian Conley, April 12, 2004, Guinea Road Cemetery file, Virginia Room, Fairfax City Regional Library.
30. Kerri Barile, email message to Brian Conley, May 10, 2004, Guinea Road Cemetery file, Virginia Room, Fairfax City Regional Library.
31. Brian Conley, email message to Kerri Barile, May 14, 2004, Guinea Road Cemetery file, Virginia Room, Fairfax City Regional Library.

32. Kerri Barile to Kathleen Kirkpatrick, May 27, 2004, Guinea Road Cemetery file, Virginia Room, Fairfax City Regional Library.

33. Dennis Howard to Mark Warner, June 11, 2004, Guinea Road Cemetery file, Virginia Room, Fairfax City Regional Library.

34. Douglas Owsley and Malcolm Richardson to Kathleen Kirkpatrick, June 16, 2004, Guinea Road Cemetery file, Virginia Room, Fairfax City Regional Library.

35. Fairfax County Minute Book 1807, 30, from Debbie Robison, "Guinea Road Cemetery: Chain of Key Events," unpublished research paper, n.d.

36. Fairfax County Minute Book 1809, 12, from Debbie Robison, "Guinea Road Cemetery: Chain of Key Events," n.d.

37. Fairfax County Deed Book Q3(69): 551, from Debbie Robison, "Guinea Road Cemetery: Chain of Key Events," n.d.

38. Fairfax County Deed Book Q3(69): 489, from Debbie Robison, "Guinea Road Cemetery: Chain of Key Events," n.d.

39. "Fairfax County School District Boundaries," *Fairfax Herald*, July 4, 1930, 4.

40. Fairfax County Deed Book 1603, p. 529.

41. Gary Farrell to Dennis Howard, August 17, 2004, Guinea Road Cemetery file, Virginia Room, Fairfax City Regional Library.

42. John Kelly, "With a Bit of Digging, Past Is Unearthed," *Washington Post*, April 25, 2006, B3.

43. Williams, "Guinea Road/Little River Turnpike Cemetery."

44. Louis Berger Group Inc., *Data Recovery at Guinea Road Cemetery Site (Site 44FX1664) Route 236 (Little River Turnpike)* (Richmond: Virginia Department of Transportation, March 2009), 135.

45. Louis Berger Group Inc., *Data Recovery at Guinea Road Cemetery Site*, 4.

46. Kelly, "With a Bit of Digging, Past Is Unearthed," B3.

7. Preservation

1. John Kelly, "With a Bit of Digging, the Past Is Unearthed," *Washington Post*, April 25, 2006, B3.

2. Andy Williams, email message to Malcolm Richardson, October 22, 2004, personal files of Maddy McCoy.

3. Malcolm Richardson, email message to Brian Conley, October 27, 2004, Guinea Road Cemetery file, Virginia Room, Fairfax City Regional Library.

4. "Happy Holidays" card from Dennis Howard to Brian Conley, n.d., Guinea Road Cemetery file, Virginia Room, Fairfax City Regional Library.

5. Dennis Howard to Andrew Williams, January 5, 2005, Guinea Road Cemetery file, Virginia Room, Fairfax City Regional Library.

6. Brian Conley to Dennis Howard, January 20, 2005, Guinea Road Cemetery file, Virginia Room, Fairfax City Regional Library.

7. Louis Berger Group Inc., *Cemetery Testing: Guinea Road Cemetery (44FX1664) Route 236 (Little River Turnpike),* February 2005, 8.

8. Louis Berger Group Inc., *Data Recovery at Guinea Road Cemetery Site (Site 44FX1664) Route 236 (Little River Turnpike)* (Richmond: Virginia Department of Transportation, March 2009), 26.

9. Kerri Barile, email message to Brian Conley, January 21, 2005, Guinea Road Cemetery file, Virginia Room, Fairfax City Regional Library.

10. Dennis Howard to Brian Conley, February 12, 2005.

11. John E. Muse (district environmental manager, Virginia Department of Transportation) to Dennis Howard, March 2, 2005, personal files of Maddy McCoy.

12. Kerri Barile to Kathleen S. Kilpatrick (director, Office of Review and Compliance, Virginia Department of Historic Resources), March 28, 2005, personal files of Maddy McCoy.

13. Draft of letter from Douglas Owsley to Kathleen S. Kilpatrick (director, Office of Review and Compliance, Virginia Department of Historic Resources), April 25, 2005, personal files of Maddy McCoy.

14. This and subsequent references to the meeting are from "Minutes: Route 236/Guinea Road, Section 106 Consulting Parties Meeting," VDOT #0236-029-120, UPC: 17671; VDHR #2004-0680, June 3, 2005, personal files of Maddy McCoy.

15. Alec MacGillis, "A Tribute to Forgotten Souls Saved from the Bulldozer," *Washington Post,* October 1, 2006, C3.

16. Michael Zwelling, "Dearly Departed Make Way for Roadwork," *Washington Examiner,* January 20, 2006, 3.

17. "Paving over the Dead," *Preservation,* July/August 2005, 14.

18. "Memorandum of Agreement among the Federal Highway Administration, the Virginia State Historic Preservation Officer, and the Virginia Department of Transportation Regarding Improvements to Route 236, Fairfax County, Va.," February 21, 2006, in appendix A to Louis Berger Group Inc., *Data Recovery at Guinea Road Cemetery Site (Site 44FX1664) Route 236 (Little River Turnpike)* (Richmond: Virginia Department of Transportation, March 2009), 161.

19. Final Order, *Commonwealth Transportation Commissioner of Virginia v. Dennis Howard,* Chancery No. 2005 5840, February 24, 2006.

20. This and subsequent references to the Berger excavation are from Louis Berger Group Inc., *Data Recovery at Guinea Road Cemetery Site (Site 44FX1664) Route 236 (Little River Turnpike)* (Richmond: Virginia Department of Transportation, March 2009).
21. Louis Berger Group Inc., *Data Recovery at Guinea Road Cemetery Site*, 135.
22. Virginia Department of Transportation, *Bulletin*, 2006.
23. "An Historic Task at Little River Turnpike and Guinea Road," Truro Trails, Truro Homes Association, October 23, 2004, 5.
24. Maddy McCoy, interview by the author, January 21, 2022.
25. Brian Conley to Dennis Howard, May 24, 2006, Guinea Road Cemetery file, Virginia Room, Fairfax City Regional Library.
26. Dennis Howard to Brian Conley, June 6, 2006, personal files of Maddy McCoy.
27. Brian Conley comments to Jack Hiller, chairman, Historical Marker Committee, Fairfax County History Commission, June 6, 2006, Guinea Road Cemetery file, Virginia Room, Fairfax City Regional Library.
28. Weather Underground, historic weather from Reagan National Airport readings, September 30, 2006.
29. "A Family Burial," *Fairfax Connection*, October 5, 2006.
30. Alec MacGillis, "A Tribute to Forgotten Souls Saved from the Bulldozer," *Washington Post*, October 1, 2006, C3.
31. Brian Conley, email message to John P. Cooke, VDOT archaeologist, October 3, 2006, Guinea Road Cemetery file, Virginia Room, Fairfax City Regional Library.
32. "A Family Burial," *Fairfax Connection*, October 5, 2006, http://www.connectionnewspapers.com/news/2006/oct/05/a-family-burial/.
33. John Kelly, "Preparing for the Future by Honoring the Past," *Washington Post*, April 27, 2006, B3.
34. Andy Williams, email message to multiple recipients, October 4, 2006, Guinea Road Cemetery file, Virginia Room, Fairfax City Regional Library.
35. "Possible Threats against Road Project Investigated," WTOPnews.com, Guinea Road Cemetery file, Virginia Room, City of Fairfax Regional Library.
36. *Save the Guinea Road Graveyard* flier, personal files of Maddy McCoy.
37. Louis Berger Group Inc., *Data Recovery at Guinea Road Cemetery*.
38. Dennis Howard, memorandum to Mary Lipsey, June 9, 2008, Guinea Road Cemetery file, Virginia Room, Fairfax City Regional Library.
39. John Cooke to Kathleen Kilpatrick, November 23, 2010, Guinea Road Cemetery file, Virginia Room, Fairfax City Regional Library.

8. Redemption

1. Weather Underground report for December 19, 2010.
2. "Ilda/Guinea Road Cemetery Sign Dedication–December 2010," Fairfax County Cemetery Preservation Association, January 6, 2011.
3. Louis Berger Group Inc., *Data Recovery at Guinea Road Cemetery Site (Site 44FX1664) Route 236 (Little River Turnpike)* (Richmond: Virginia Department of Transportation, March 2009), 131.
4. Louis Berger Group Inc., *Data Recovery at Guinea Road Cemetery Site*, 132.
5. Louis Berger Group Inc., *Data Recovery at Guinea Road Cemetery Site*, 133–34.
6. Maddy McCoy, email message to Jack Hiller, chairman, Fairfax County History Commission, August 31, 2009, Fairfax County History Commission files, Virginia Room, Fairfax City Regional Library.
7. Christina Sturdivant, "Anti-Semitic Graffiti Found at Jewish Community Center and Church in Fairfax," *DCist*, April 11, 2017, https://dcist.com/story/17/04/11/jcc-vandalism/.
8. "About," Little River United Church of Christ website, https://www.lrucc.org/about.
9. "Slave History near LRUCC," Little River United Church of Christ website, https://static1.squarespace.com/static /5a4c0633914e6b17448f8f17/t/5aeb6622562fa7a9b2481c07 /1525376547915/slaveHistoryNearLRUCC.pdf.
10. "Plan and Profile of Proposed State Highway, Fairfax County, Little River Turnpike and Guinea Road Intersection Improvements," Virginia Department of Transportation, January 2021, 5.
11. "Little River Turnpike/Guinea Road Intersection Improvements: Virtual Information Meeting," March 1, 2021.
12. "Little River Turnpike and Guinea Road Intersection Improvements: Public Involvement Summary," Virginia Department of Transportation, 7.
13. Lynn Rainville, *Hidden History: African American Cemeteries in Central Virginia* (Charlottesville: University of Virginia Press, 2014), 95.
14. Rainville, *Hidden History*, 96.
15. Ryan K. Smith, *Death and Rebirth in a Southern City: Richmond's Historic Cemeteries* (Baltimore, MD: Johns Hopkins University Press, 2020), 2.
16. Smith, *Death and Rebirth in a Southern City*, 59–65.
17. Smith, *Death and Rebirth in a Southern City*, 115.
18. Contrabands and Freedmen Cemetery Memorial website, City of Alexandria, https://www.alexandriava.gov/FreedmenMemorial.

19. Daniella Cheslow, "In Virginia, a Family Tragedy Stirs New Life in a Burial Ground for the Enslaved," NPR Station WAMU 88.5, August 28, 2020, https://www.npr.org/local/305/2020/08/28/907003159/in-virginia-a-family-tragedy-stirs-new-life-in-a-burial-ground-for-the-enslaved.
20. Rebecca Tan, "At a Historic Cemetery for the Enslaved, a Mother's Personal Grief Mixes with Collective Mourning," *Washington Post,* October 24, 2021, https://www.washingtonpost.com/dc-md-va/2021/10/24/loudoun-enslaved-burial-ground-belmont-virginia/.
21. Theresa Vargas, "While Working to Restore Two Historic Black Cemeteries, She Discovered a Construction Crew Digging on Burial Grounds," *Washington Post,* October 9, 2021, https://www.washingtonpost.com/dc-md-va/2021/10/24/loudoun-enslaved-burial-ground-belmont-virginia/.
22. S. 3667, https://www.congress.gov/bill/117th-congress/senate-bill/3667/text.
23. "Fairfax County Confederate Names Inventory Report," Fairfax County History Commission, December 8, 2020, 7–8, https://www.fairfaxcounty.gov/history-commission/sites/history-commission/files/assets/documents/confederate-names-committee/confederate-names-inventory-report.pdf.
24. Matt Blitz, "Fairfax County to Honor Black History with Six New Historical Markers," September 19, 2022, https://www.ffxnow.com/2022/09/19/fairfax-county-to-honor-black-history-with-six-new-historical-markers/
25. "Braddock District Black History Month: Slavery in the Braddock District," February 2021, https://www.fairfaxcounty.gov/braddock/braddock-district-black-history-month.
26. Badil-Abish, *Shades of Gray,* 68.
27. Rev. Paul Shepard, interview by the author, January 20, 2022.
28. Douglas Dove, oral history interview by Dan Cragg, September 18 and 25, 1993, Virginia Room, Fairfax City Regional Library.

Acknowledgments

1. Hareem Badil-Abish, *Shades of Gray: A Beginning . . . The Origins and Development of a Black Family in Virginia* (Estate of Hareem Badil-Abish, 2005).
2. Dennis Howard to Brian Conley, February 12, 2005, Guinea Road Cemetery file, Virginia Room, Fairfax City Regional Library.

BIBLIOGRAPHY

Official Records

Fairfax County Board of Supervisors Meeting Minutes
Fairfax County Board of Zoning Appeals Minute Books
Fairfax County Chancery Court Records
Fairfax County Circuit Court Historic Records
Fairfax County Circuit Court Minute Books
Fairfax County Circuit Court Term Papers
Fairfax County Comprehensive Plan, 1991
Fairfax County Deed Books
Fairfax County Historical Imagery Viewer
Fairfax County Personal Property Tax Records
Fairfax County Planning Commission Meeting Minutes
Fairfax County School Board Meeting Minutes
Fairfax County Will Books
Falls Church District School Board Minutes
U.S. Census, 1870, 1880

Subject Files, Virginia Room, City of Fairfax Regional Library

Annandale
Guinea Road Cemetery
Ilda

Little River Turnpike
Merrifield
Oak Hill
Ravensworth
Wakefield Chapel

Oral History Interviews

Dobbins, Marion. Interview by Linda Byrne for the Providence District History Project. January 21, 2008.

Dove, Douglas. Interview by Dan Cragg. September 18 and 25, 1993.

Hill, Avonjeannette "Dolly." Interview by Naomi Sokol Zeavin. 2005.

Howard, Dennis. Interview by Ira Andrews. April 14, 2008. Macon Memories Oral History Project, Randolph-Macon College. 2008. https://www.youtube.com/watch?v=NsjQYD8IFL4.

———. Interview by Mary Lipsey. August 15, 2005. https://braddockheritage.org/archive/files /d6774c756c4445e9548d89809ec6db03.pdf.

Keith, Judge James. Interview by Karen Coleman. March 11, 1974. Virginia Room, Fairfax City Regional Library.

Packard, Jean. Interview by Margaret Shuler. May 2, 2005.

Robey, Everett. Interview by Jennifer Santley. Deposited at Northern Virginia Folklife Center, George Mason University, 1981–82.

Wakefield, Lowell. Interview by D'Anne Evans. December 9, 1976.

West, William A. Interview by C. J. S. Durham and Mrs. Charles Rieger for the Fairfax County History Commission. September 17, 1974.

Wright, Aileen. Interview by Mary Lipsey for the Providence District History Project. October 25, 2007.

Interviews by the Author

Bulova, Sharon. August 13, 2021.

Clark, Jeff. February 21, 2023.

McCoy, Maddy. January 21, 2022.

Shepard, Rev. Dr. Paul. January 20, 2022.

Walkinshaw, James. August 6, 2021.

Periodicals

Alexandria Gazette
Burke Connection
Fairfax Connection
Fairfax Herald

Herndon Observer
Northern Virginia Sun
Richmond Planet
Washington Evening Star
Washington Post

Other Sources

Badil-Abish, Hareem. *Shades of Gray: A Beginning . . . The Origins and Development of a Black Family in Virginia*. Estate of Hareem Badil-Abish, 2005.

Banham, Russ. *The Fight for Fairfax: Private Citizens and Public Policymaking*. Fairfax, VA: George Mason University Press, 2020.

Berlin, Ira. *Slaves without Masters: The Free Negro in the Antebellum South*. New York: New Press, 2007.

Browne, John. *The Story of Ravensworth*. Scott's Valley, CA: CreateSpace Independent Publishing Platform, 2018.

Burks, Harry Hunter, Jr. "The Development of the Public Elementary School System of Fairfax County, Virginia from the School Year 1927–28 through the School Year 1941–42." Master's thesis in education, Duke University, 1942.

Citizen's Handbook of Fairfax County. Fairfax, VA: County of Fairfax, 1964.

Conley, Brian A. *Return to Union: Fairfax County's Role in the Adoption of the Virginia Constitution of 1870*. Fairfax, VA: Fairfax County Public Library, 2001.

"Contrabands and Freedmen Cemetery Memorial." City of Alexandria website. https://www.alexandriava.gov/FreedmenMemorial.

A County Called Fairfax: Being a Student's Digest of Our Government and History. Fairfax, VA: Fairfax County Office of the County Executive, 1966.

Epps, Garrett. "Want to Know More about Critical Race Theory? Look at Virginia's Schools—For More Than 75 Years." *Washington Monthly*, October 25, 2021.

Evans, D'Anne A. *Wakefield Chapel*. Fairfax, VA: Fairfax County Office of Comprehensive Planning, 1977.

"Fairfax City Cemetery History." City of Fairfax website. https://www.fairfaxva.gov/government/public-works/operations-division/cemetery/cemetery-s-history.

Fairfax County Confederate Names Inventory Report. Fairfax, VA: Fairfax County History Commission, 2020. https://www.fairfax county.gov/history-commission/sites/history-commission/files/assets/documents/confederate-names-committee/confederate-names-inventory-report.pdf.

Fairfax County 2007 Community Citizen Planning Committee. *Fairfax County Stories: 1607–2007.* Fairfax, VA: County of Fairfax, Virginia, 2007.

Gutheim, Frederick. *A History Program for Fairfax County.* Fairfax, VA: Fairfax County Park Authority, 1973.

Harrison, Fairfax. *Landmarks of Old Prince William: A Study of Origins in Northern Virginia.* Richmond, VA: Old Dominion Press, 1924.

An Historic Task at Little River Turnpike and Guinea Road. Truro Trails, Truro Homes Association, 2004.

History of Fairfax County, Virginia. Fairfax, VA: Department of Education, Fairfax County, 1957.

"History of Pozez JCC of Northern Virginia." Pozez JCC of Northern Virginia website. https://www.thej.org/about/about/.

Hogan, K. S. *Centennial Chronicle of Fairfax County Public Schools, Commonwealth of Virginia, 1870–1970.* N.d.

Hopkins, G. M. *Atlas of Fifteen Miles around Washington, D.C.* Philadelphia: G. M. Hopkins, 1878.

Howrey, Edward. *Washington Lawyer.* Iowa City: University of Iowa College of Law, 1983.

Industrial Sketch of Fairfax County, Virginia. Fairfax, VA: Fairfax County Board of Supervisors, 1907.

Jamieson, Ross W. "Material Culture and Social Death: African-American Burial Practices." *Historical Archaeology* 29, no. 4 (1995).

John Milner Associates. *Fairfax County Civil War Sites Inventory.* Fairfax, VA: Fairfax County Park Authority, 2002. https://www .fairfaxcounty.gov/parks/sites/parks/files/assets/documents /naturalcultural/civil%20war%20inventory.pdf.

Johnson, William Page. *Brothers and Cousins: Confederate Soldiers and Sailors of Fairfax County, Virginia.* Athens, GA: Iberian Publishing, 1995.

Kovach Shuman, Sue. *Mantua.* Mount Pleasant, SC: Arcadia, 2021.

Louis Berger Group Inc. *Data Recovery at Guinea Road Cemetery Site (Site 44FX1664) Route 236 (Little River Turnpike).* Richmond: Virginia Department of Transportation, 2009.

Mauro, Charles. *The Civil War in Fairfax County: Civilians and Soldiers.* Cheltenham, Gloucestershire, UK: History Press, 2006.

McCarron, Kay. "An Archaeological Review of the Mondan Tract at the Intersection of Guinea Road and Little River Turnpike, Fairfax County Virginia." Unpublished paper. 1990.

McElya, Micki. *The Politics of Mourning: Death and Honor in Arlington National Cemetery.* Cambridge, MA: Harvard University Press, 2016.

Meany, Marion, and Mary Lipsey. *Braddock's True Gold: 20th Century Life in the Heart of Fairfax County.* Fairfax, VA: County of Fairfax, 2007.

Bibliography

Miller, John Chester. *The Wolf by the Ears: Thomas Jefferson and Slavery.* New York: Free Press, 1977.

Netherton, Nan, and Ross Netherton. *Fairfax County: A Contemporary Portrait.* Virginia Beach, VA: Donning, 1992.

Netherton, Nan, Donald Sweig, Janice Artemel, Patricia Hinkin, and Patrick Reed. *Fairfax County, Virginia: A History.* Fairfax, VA: Fairfax County Board of Supervisors, 1978.

Owsley, Douglas. "Report of Survey, Archaeological Site 44FX1664." Unpublished paper. 1991.

"Paving over the Dead." *Preservation,* July/August 2005.

Pine Ridge Park: Master Plan Amendment. Fairfax, VA: Fairfax County Park Authority, 2007.

Rainville, Lynn. *Hidden History: African American Cemeteries in Central Virginia.* Charlottesville: University of Virginia Press, 2014.

Robison, Debbie. "Guinea Road Cemetery: Chain of Key Events." Unpublished research report. N.d.

———. "List of Blacks in Fairfax County, VA, 1866–69, Based on Personal Property Tax Records." Northern Virginia History Notes website. http://www.novahistory.org/Fairfax_Blacks_1866-1869/Fairfax_Blacks_1866-1869.htm.

Russell, John Henderson. "The Free Negro in Virginia 1619–1865." PhD diss., Johns Hopkins University, 1913.

"Slave History near LRUCC." Little River United Church of Christ website. https://static1.squarespace.com/static/5a4c0633914e6b17448f8f17/t/5aeb6622562fa7a9b2481c07/1525376547915/slaveHistoryNearLRUCC.pdf.

Smith, Ryan K. *Death and Rebirth in a Southern City: Richmond's Historic Cemeteries.* Baltimore, MD: Johns Hopkins University Press, 2020.

Sobel, Mechal. *The World They Made Together: Black and White Values in Eighteenth Century Virginia.* Princeton, NJ: Princeton University Press, 1987.

Sokol Zeavin, Naomi, and the Fairfax County History Commission, comps. "African American History in Mason District." Fairfax, VA: Fairfax County History Commission, 2005.

Thorp, Daniel. *Facing Freedom: An African American Community in Virginia from Reconstruction to Jim Crow.* Charlottesville: University of Virginia Press, 2017.

United States Department of Agriculture Bureau of Public Roads and Ford Motor Company. *The Road to Happiness.* Film. 1924.

United States War Department. *The War of the Rebellion: A Compilation of the Official Records of the Union and Confederate Armies.* Washington, DC: US Government Printing Office, 1880–1901.

Bibliography

Vaughn, Curtis L. "Freedom Is Not Enough: African Americans in Antebellum Fairfax County." PhD diss., George Mason University, 2008.

Williams, Emily. *Stories in Stone.* Wilmington, DE: Vernon, 2020.

Wolf, Andrew M. D. *Black Settlement in Fairfax County during Reconstruction.* Research study. Fairfax, VA: Fairfax County Office of Strategic Planning, 1975.

INDEX

Index

Index

Index

seizure of property in, 95–96; settlement of, 94–95
Pizza Hut, 91
plantations, 10, 13, 20, 42, 112–13
Pleasant Valley Memorial Park, 18, 157, 163–67
Plessy v. Ferguson, 63
poll tax, 71
Prosperity Avenue, 82, 90, 188
Providence, 15

Quakers, 29–30
Quantico National Cemetery, 177–78

racial covenants, 98–99
Radford University, 161
Rainville, Lynn, 51, 179–80
Randolph-Macon College, 106–7
Ravensworth, 8: enslaved people at, 9; Fitzhugh family at, 9, 42, 165; Gooding family at, 18; lack of school for Black children, 67; Lee family at, 13, 76; Newmans at, 12, 42; reliance on tobacco, 8; shopping center, 9
rebel yell, 76
Reconstruction, 41–43, 70, 125
registration of free African Americans, 27–28, 71, 113
Republican Party, 64–65, 116
Richardson, Malcolm: examination of Guinea Road Cemetery, 130–31; interpretation of results, 138–39, 144, 148–49, 154
Richmond, Virginia, 180–81
Richmond Planet, 72
Rinehart, Charles, 161, 167
roads: condition of, 41, 60–62, 81–82; importance to development, 14–16, 69, 91, 115–16; maintenance, 38, 60, 139; petitions to discontinue, 38; traffic issues, 121, 133, 135
roadside motels, 23
Road to Happiness, The (film), 81

Robey, Everett, 61–62, 66–67, 188
Robinson, Emma, 44
Roosevelt, Franklin, 80
Roosevelt, Teddy, 94
Roots, 113
Rupnik, Megan: archival research on Ilda, 152, 163, 173; discovery of reference to "old cemetery" at Ilda, 149
Russell, John Henderson, 27
Rutherford, John, 195
Rutherford Civic Association, 120–21

Salvation Army, 100, 126, 140
school boards, 63–67, 83, 95–96, 103, 114
schools: depiction of slavery and Civil War in textbooks, 112–13; desegregation of, 102–4; segregation of, 62–68, 87, 103, 112; teachers' salaries, 65, 88. *See also* Ilda School; Flint Hill School; Luther Jackson High School; massive resistance; Merrifield Colored School; Stratford Junior High School
Schudel, Donald, 125
Scott, Ada, 106
Seale, Bobby, 107
Second Baptist Church of Falls Church, 30, 60–61, 164, 177
Sewell, Jeanette, 46
Sewell, William H., 33, 46
sex, 120
Shepard, Rev. Paul, 62, 186
Shirley Highway, 91–92
Shockoe Bottom (Richmond neighborhood), 180–81
shooting: of Elijah Cleveland, 55–57; of Thomas Edwards, 20; of Horace Gibson, 1–2, 72–73; of John Mosby, 20–21; of road construction equipment, 2–3, 168; threat against Horace Gibson, 49
shopping centers, 9, 90, 93